THE LAST PROPHET AND JUDGE
OF THE TWELVE TRIBES OF THE CHILDREN OF ISRAEL

THE LAST PROPHET

AND JUDGE OF THE TWELVE TRIBES OF THE CHILDREN OF ISRAEL

WRITTEN AND EDITED,

BY

DALE LAWSON

LAST DAYS PRESS

SAN DIEGO

Last Days Press
P.O. Box 83657
San Diego, California 92138

Copyright © 2009 by Dale Lawson
All rights reserved,
including the right of reproduction
in whole or in part in any form.

First Last Days Press Edition, August, 2009
Manufactured in the United States of America

No part of this book may be reproduced or utilized in any form,
or by any means, without the written permission of the Publisher.
Permissions, constituting a continuation of the copyright page, are
listed on pages 359 & 360. Cover Art & Symbols used under license.

This work is registered in the United States Copyright Office, all rights
protected under International and Pan-American Copyright Conventions.

Last Days Press ™ does not participate in, endorse, or have any authority
or responsibility concerning private business transactions
between our authors and the public

Library of Congress Control Number: 2009905368

ISBN: 978-0-615-31358-0
      978-0-615-30591-2 (Pbk)

Except in the United States of America,
this book is sold subject to the condition
that it shall not, by way of trade or otherwise,
be lent, re-sold, hired out, or otherwise circulated
without the publisher's prior consent in any form of
binding or cover other than that in which it is
published and without a similar condition
including this condition being imposed
on the subsequent purchaser

The scanning, uploading and distribution of this book
via the Internet or via any other means without the permission
of the publisher is illegal and punishable by law

BOOK DESIGN BY DALE LAWSON

Dedicated to the Human Race the Flesh and Blood Heroes and to the Overcomers...

"The scepter shall not depart from Judah,
Nor a lawgiver from between his feet, until Shiloh come;
And unto him *shall* the gathering of the people *be*."

- Genesis 49: 10

"Blow ye the trumpet in Zion,
And sound an alarm in my holy mountain:
Let all the inhabitants of the land tremble:
For the day of the Lord cometh, for *it is* nigh at hand."

- Joel 2: 1

"This know also,
That in the last days perilous times shall come."

- 2 Timothy 3: 1

FORWARD

WITH the exception of the "*Holy Bible*," there are few books that can claim to have something for everyone! This book you are holding in your hands has something for everyone, of this I am certain.

This book is not free. It has a price, and that price is a genuine interest in its revelation. This is not a coffee table book, and as such, it should be prized and safeguarded. This book is not to be lent or traded or re-sold. It is unique to each individual who possesses that genuine interest in its revelation. Its gifts, rewards and knowledge are equally unique to its legitimate owner.

In other words, the gifts, rewards and knowledge herein will be conveyed to the buyer of the book, while the gifts, rewards and knowledge will be withheld from any who fail to acquire their own legitimate copy of the book, they thereby lacking that genuine interest in its revelation. There will be no "Robbers of God" of this revelation or of its rewards ever!

Therefore, if you are reading this book, and you have not purchased your own legitimate and unique copy, I urge you to stop-off reading right now and obtain your own personal copy of this book, so that you may receive your own unique and irreplaceable gifts, rewards and knowledge thereof, and reserve your rightful place on the "All Saints Bandwagon" out of this finishing earth!

Author's Note

IF the grid of life is a puzzle to be assembled, then human understanding is the key to its completion. This book is the heroic attempt to complete that puzzle. "Sir Isaac Newton, was certain that not only the Bible, but the entire universe, was a "cryptogram set by the Almighty," a puzzle that God made, and that we were meant to solve," and in so doing, to shed light on the true significance of our existence. Isaac Newton was more of a genius than any of us imagined. The universal grid is loaded with "cryptograms" that play off each other throughout eternity.

It just so happens, that within that grid a "superior element" is operating that is the all determining factor of our existence. That "superior element" is made known to all men through the book of the "*Holy Bible.*" Therefore, the key to man's understanding of himself, and of his surroundings lay buried within the pages of the "*Holy Bible.*" Man cannot find the true meaning of his existence outside of the "Book of Life," and any attempt to do so will be futile!

"Behold, I lay in Sion a chief corner stone, elect, precious:
And he that believeth on him shall not be confounded."

- 1 Peter 2: 6

This book is particularly relevant for the inhabitants of present day earth. If knowledge is power, then this writing should empower you in the right direction.

It is meant to be read slowly, deliberately as if one were searching for something of great import, but is not sure where it will be found. As the revelation of each chapter builds upon the preceding one, it has to be read from beginning to end otherwise you'll miss the gift. It is best read during your quiet time, when you are unhurried, and uninterrupted, when all the pieces come together.

This manuscript is a journey through the trials, and tribulations of a soul who is trying to find its origin, its Creator, its purpose. That said, portions of it are written in the first person. Although the experiences, insights, and discoveries are those of its author, it is written for every man and woman.

Whenever the term "Man" is used, it signifies every man, or every woman, and has nothing to do with gender.

Whenever the term "Israelite" is used, it signifies every man, or every woman, who has acknowledged and accepted the divinity in man, and thus, has accepted the Almighty. It specifically refers to those who are the true descendants of the "Twelve Tribes of the Children of Israel," regardless of their race today. It further denotes those who are the "Salt of the Earth," and those who are the true "Light-Bearers" of the world, the "Lights of Israel" if you would. In essence, the true heirs of Abraham, Isaac, and Jacob. It does not necessarily refer to all members of the Jewish race, or to the Jewish nation as a whole. There are many in the Jewish race that have denied the Almighty, and have therefore been converted into the ranks of the true Philistines.

Whenever the term "Philistine" is used, it signifies every man, or every woman, who has ignored and denied the divinity in man, and thus, has denied the Almighty. It implies the smug atheists in all walks of life who have had the arrogance to use the "Gift of Life" that the Almighty has afforded them, while denying him at the same time. It especially means those who have ceaselessly warred against the children of God since the beginning of the Human Race. It does not necessarily refer to all members of the Palestinian race, or to the Palestine nation as a whole. There are many in the Palestinian race that have accepted the Almighty, and have therefore been converted into the ranks of the true Israelites.

This work and the experiences herein, serve to corroborate that the warnings of the "*Holy Bible*" are true, and thus, should not be ignored!

The Maltese cross is a strong spiritual symbol despite its misuse. It is restored in this manuscript to its true spiritual significance.

You will find many styles of writing as you make your way through. Each chapter is unique, and stands on its own. The structures of the chapters are designed for maximum impact of the subject presented. The lines are just long enough or short enough to enhance or empower the idea. The sections are compressed, words and expressions are tightly knit, and chosen to be the shortest distance between two points, or two poles of thought. It attempts to extract the most out of language, by using the most pertinent words, and phrases, to allow the greatest imagery. Its aim is to encapsulate the spirit of what is being imparted with full integrity and minimum ambiguity. It is the only way all the pieces of the puzzle will fit.

The punctuation is meant to accentuate its rhythm and pitch, rather than be grammatically precise. Its commas are placed, or timed, for you to take a moment of thought, and reflection, before continuing on. Its exclamation marks are used to proclaim a truth, or a revelation that is being unmasked! Its quotation marks are utilized to call attention to "important concepts" that should be examined. The ellipsis is used when I want you to continue the thought, or ponder the consequences....

The Pieces of the Puzzle

Preface		xiii
Introduction		xv
1.	The Human Race	21
2.	The Veiled Mind	22
3.	The Clouded Mind	23
4.	The Dual Nature of Man	24
5.	The Affliction	25
6.	The Illusory Dream	26
7.	The Prodigal Path	27
8.	The Lost Soul	28
9.	The Divine Conviction	29
10.	The Laws of Life	30
11.	The Beat of Life	31
12.	The Hum of Life	32
13.	The Mirror Image	33
14.	The Base of Creation	34
15.	The Creator's Clock	35
16.	The Vine of Life	36
17.	The Main Gate	37
18.	The Wedding Day	38
19.	The Day of Rapture	39
20.	The Gift of Life	40
21.	The Gift of Innocence	41
22.	The Day of Initiation	42
23.	The Baptism of Fire	43
24.	The Holy Communion	44
25.	The Hallowed Child	45
26.	The Spiritual Mind	46
27.	The Carnal Mind	47
28.	The Fall from Grace	48
29.	The Temptation	49
30.	The Crossroads of Life	50
31.	The Coin of the Realm	51
32.	The Rod of Obedience	52
33.	The Key to Reparation	53
34.	The Realization of Truth	54

35.	The Key to Harmony	55
36.	The Measure of a Man	56
37.	The Considerate	57
38.	The Divine Immunity	58
39.	The Grace of God	59
40.	The Whited Sepulchers	60
41.	The Temples of Ruin	61
42.	The Valley of Bones	62
43.	The Living and the Dead	63
44.	The Voice in the Wilderness	64
45.	The Barren Fields	65
46.	The False Virtues	66
47.	The False Values	67
48.	The Pure Advantage	68
49.	The Absolution of Sin	69
50.	The Pure Genius	70
51.	The Moderate Man	71
52.	The Eternal Treasure	72
53.	The Will of Man	73
54.	The Will of God	74
55.	The Finite Mind	75
56.	The Infinite Mind	76
57.	The Spiral Staircase	77
58.	The Positive and Negative	79
59.	The Burden of Density	81
60.	The Planes of Desire	82
61.	The Scales of Justice	84
62.	The Waves of Karma	85
63.	The Crucible of Time	86
64.	The Inexperienced Man	87
65.	The Experienced Man	89
66.	The Immature Soul	91
67.	The Mature Soul	93
68.	The Sacred Sound	94
69.	The Stir of Enchantment	97
70.	The Unnatural Mind	98
71.	The Wheel of Mind	99
72.	The Natural Mind	100
73.	The Turnabout	101
74.	The Separation	102
75.	The Separate Self	103
76.	The Microcosmic Self	105
77.	The Macrocosmic Self	106
78.	The Master's Vessel	107
79.	The Master	108

80.	The Assessment	109
81.	The Mortal Grid	110
82.	The Immortal Grid	111
83.	The Puzzle	112
84.	The Message	113
85.	The Messenger	114
86.	The Rigid	115
87.	The Fearful	116
88.	The Day of Judgment	119
89.	The Day of Desolation	122
90.	The Evildoer and the Liar	123
91.	The Blessing and the Curse	124
92.	The True Israelite	125
93.	The Discriminator	126
94.	The Division	127
95.	The Sword of Truth	129
96.	The Hardened	130
97.	The Needful	131
98.	The Abusers	132
99.	The Stream	133
100.	The Unjust Stewards	134
101.	The Temple	135
102.	The Soul	136
103.	The Dyad	137
104.	The Shepherd	138
105.	The Herd	139
106.	The Hollow	140
107.	The Thread	141
108.	The Rod of Iron	142
109.	The Wellspring	144
110.	The Morning Star	145
111.	The King of Kings	146
112.	The Twelve Tribes of Israel	152
113.	The Israelites and the Philistines	154
114.	The Burning Cell	158
115.	The Persecution	162
116.	The Crucifixion	163
117.	The Flame	164
118.	The Death	165
119.	The Sorrow	166
120.	The Breath of Life	167
121.	The Resurrection	168
122.	The Fallen Angels	169
123.	The Last Antichrists	170
124.	The End of Days	171

125.	The False Prophet	172
126.	The Battle of Armageddon	173
127.	The Seven Headed Beast	175
128.	The Man and the Machine	176
129.	The Flesh and Blood Hero	177
130.	The Red Dragons of Death	178
131.	The Four Horsemen of the Apocalypse	179
132.	The Tremors of Tribulation	180
133.	The Ascent to the Summit	182
134.	The Rescue of the Remnant	184
135.	The Wake of Destruction	185
136.	The Mountain of God	186
137.	The Sealed Book	187
138.	The Unsealed Book	188
139.	The Inner Vision	191
140.	The Law Divine	192
141.	The Power Supreme	193
142.	The Blessing of Israel	194
143.	The True Human	195
144.	The Crown of Life	196

Coda	197
Afterthought	198
Definitions and Terms	201
Reference Scripture	203
Permissions, Citations & Acknowledgments	359

Preface

IF the being of man can be likened to a plant, and the human family to a garden, then it pays to be a gardener. The knowledge and techniques of gardening would be vital to the human condition, just to keep it from wasting away.

Any farmer knows there is a time to sow the seed, and a time to reap the harvest. The harvest cannot be put off indefinitely, or it will surely be lost.

This book is a harvesting tool, to gather up the people, and help maximize the yield before the entire field is plowed under!

Dale Lawson

Southern, California

August 2009

INTRODUCTION

THIS is a timely book. It is the Author's firm conviction that we are living in the "End of Days" as foretold in the "*Holy Bible.*" It is likewise believed that the present generation inhabiting our planet will soon experience the climactic conflagration known as the "Battle of Armageddon." As the first "Heaven and Earth" is rolled up as a scroll, the grand finale of the entire human experiment will result in a wholly new creation. If indeed, we are living in the "End of Days," what could be timelier?

"Behold, I will send you Elijah the prophet
Before the coming of the great and dreadful day of the Lord."

- Malachi 4: 5

This is an absolute book, in the sense that it is pure unvarnished truth, and that it is complete and will unconditionally accomplish that which it sets out to do. It is also a peculiar book, in the sense that it is uncommon and nonconforming to the world's standards. The Human Race needs this message now in order to properly traverse the spiritual crossroads looming on the horizon, and that are already here.

The message herein has merit, it works on several levels, and it might just be the most unique, compelling, and profound book of its kind. That said, it can be read simply as a testimony of the human soul. It can be read as an instruction manual for the human soul and its condition. And finally, it can be read thoroughly along with its "Reference Scripture," as divinely inspired prophecy, which is what it is, where you will find new meanings and depths of Biblical truth as it pertains to our human condition and to the modern world.

This is a solemn announcement that is being issued to the Human population, and serves to notify earth's inhabitants that the "Lord's Day," which is the "Day of Judgment" that has been recorded of old in the book of the "*Holy Bible*" is at hand.

It officially declares that the Human Race has reached its destination for this era, and that the entire matter is coming to a close. It is nigh time to award the Overcomers, and to sentence the guilty.

This book hereby unseals the "Book of Revelation." It opens the "Seven Seals" thereof, so that the Creator's will and its contents may be fulfilled, even unto its completion. It ushers in the "Lord's Day," and simultaneously sets the stage for the divine ending, the exodus of the remnant from the planetary body, those souls that have been redeemed from the foundation of the earth. The "Rapture" of the saints!

This message serves the Creator's purpose, and so, it came about of necessity. Between the fall of 87, and the summer of 89, the writings of this book came to me. Wherever I would happen to be, I would stop what I was doing, and right these passages down. During this period, I found these lightning bolts of information flooding into my mind in such a way that I had to write them down for fear that they would be lost. They were not so much created as captured on paper. I often found myself scribbling faster and faster just to get them down. When I had free time, I compiled them according to the dates that I wrote them down.

In early 2006, after having read *"The Bible Code"* books, I was prompted to pick up *"The Little Book"* that I had set aside. I began editing it, at which time I wrote eight final chapters, the titles of the chapters, and then added the corroborating scripture. The order in which you find them is the order in which I received them and wrote them down, with the exception of the final eight that easily fell into place.

I consider these writings to be divinely inspired and therefore, non-fiction of the highest sort. In my heart of hearts, I know the divine weight of this book.

This text reads more like a spiritual odyssey through the modern world, and after seeing the values of that world, becomes a scathing critique of it. Perhaps no passage is more revealing than the following...

"Four elements of God in balanced fusion,
Fire and air and water and earth,
The awesome power of nature uses,
For in all the myriad forms of nature,
Only man or woman abuses...."

- The Abusers

It condemns the bad or dangerous and suggests the good or beneficial. It at once reprimands those who need it, and praises those who deserve it. It places signposts and warnings for the inexperienced traveler, subtle hints to the more advanced, and blatant commands when they are the prescription for what ails you, but always with the traveler and the destination in mind.

If the temple of man is the building, and man the builder, then the knowledge of divine construction is the keystone to man's spiritual success. It is no secret that the act of constructing without applying its fundamental knowledge is a risky business. This book seeks to identify the spiritual archetypes and key elements that are the building blocks of life, so that man the builder can get on with the task at hand.

As in all building, there are indispensable pieces that must be placed at the outset. If the chief stones can be gathered from the quarry of "Human Wisdom," and then added to the "Foundation Stone," the edifice of our understanding can be erected. The "Temple of Man" can be built, which is the "Temple of God."

This book is an attempt in that direction. It seeks to elucidate the hidden mysteries of the "*Holy Bible*" as they relate to present day earth, the end time prophecies, and to the fate of humanity itself. Its purpose is to afford us a more complete understanding of Biblical truth, the Hebrew prophecies, and to the mystery of the ages, hopefully to ascertain where we stand as individuals within that context.

The goal of this work is to remove impediments from human lives, while instilling a vision that can truly improve their plight. Its aim is the betterment of humanity by using timeless spiritual truths at the most propitious time.

This is a spiritual document first and a human document last. I have always been concerned with eternal truth as it pertains to the human condition. It turns out that the human condition needs eternal truth just as much as it needs oxygen, and sunlight in order to flower and become fruitful.

Just as all souls are born into matter, learn to crawl, then walk, and exit the screen of life at the appointed time, there are fixed landmarks that each soul will encounter and pass through in time. These milestones are the key components of the very framework of life itself, the eternal grid of which we are linked.

We function as an integral part of that grid. Thus, man and matter, consciousness and existence are inextricably woven together. We complete each other, compliment each other, and play off of each other throughout eternity. It is the play of life, and we all are the performers. As fate would have it, it turns out that the play we are currently engaged in is in the final act, and the curtain is about to come down.

A soul's growth proceeds in stages, along a winding path, and there are many markers pointing the way. It is a course fraught with danger, and snares to be encountered. It has its laws as guideposts that will assist the weary traveler to the much needed safe haven, where one can gain respite. There are numerous wrong turns that can waylay you. And, there are the right turns that can hasten your crossing. This writing is the epic attempt to map that journey.

As you read through, you will encounter some Eastern concepts such as Karma, Re-embodiment, Tao and Zen. It is quite natural to me that re-embodiment is God's way of returning us until perfected. The Bible refers to it as the "Transmigration of Souls." The process of re-embodiment since the day of Abraham has resulted in the scattering of the "Twelve Tribes of Israel" over the whole earth. They reside now in every country and corner of the globe. They may have any name or belong to any race. The children of Israel know who they are by virtue of the law which was written in their hearts and minds.

Its contents, and whole intent, is to uncover truth, to "decode" truth, and present that truth to the "Twelve Tribes of the Children of Israel," and to all true believers who now comprise the inhabitants of the whole world, along with the children of Ishmael.

The sole purpose of this book is to be a witness to what is true, and represents the culmination of a soul's journey through an era, that is now at an end. It brings to completion and closes the final chapters of the sojourns of the "Twelve Tribes of the Children of Israel," as set forth in the "*Holy Bible*," this book will gather the people together prior to their mass exodus from planet earth. An earth exodus if you will!

It provides an outline, a path, an instruction, and a vision, for the true Israelites, all true believers, and those who thirst for the fountain of life, therefore, drink deeply.

May you fare thee well!

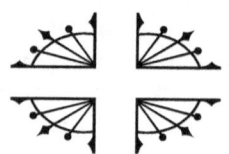

THE LAST PROPHET AND JUDGE
OF THE TWELVE TRIBES OF THE CHILDREN OF ISRAEL

Chapter 1

The Human Race

WHAT is Life...?
What is its purpose...?
What are you...?

Is this round yet another game of hide and seek?
If so, then why haven't you found?
But one must seek in order to find, and whom are you seeking?

The man made self, or the God made self?
The real self or the unreal self...?
Are you an end in itself, or a means to an end?

A means to what end...?
Are you seeking the divine within, or the world without?
Are you an heir of the seed of Abraham, or a Philistine?

Are you a child of the Twelve Tribes of Israel, or of Ishmael?
Are you a flame, or a flicker?
Are you a child of God, or not...?

Chapter 2

The Veiled Mind

THE synthetic self...,
Cast in a delusive mold,
Plays an allusive game....

Its object,
To capture the attention,
Of the unwary one!

The lure of the senses,
Entices and beckons,
The mind to its disguise....

The conceit of fashion!
The deceit of glamour!
The arrogance of prestige!

Merely thorns of seduction,
Upon which we rend,
The hem of our souls!

Chapter 3

The Clouded Mind

TOO easily,
The attention of the idle mind,
Is drawn to no good....

Lack of control, leads to the sway of the senses,
The sway of the senses leads to desire,
Desire leads to imprudent action....

Imprudent action leads to convolution, confusion and chaos,
These afflictions cause and result in..., the clouded mind,
That soon breeds guilt, separation and self-condemnation....

This lack of vigilance,
Sets us outside of the circle of Oneness....
Once divided...,

One is easily conquered,
Or swallowed, if you will...,
By shadows, and black clouds of human miscreation!

Chapter 4

The Dual Nature of Man

THE ability to affirm or praise others,
Stems from the satisfaction of ourselves,
Which at the same time, enhances
Our feeling of unity in the One....
The more we truly praise others,
The closer we are drawn to the One!

The ability to judge or condemn others,
Stems from the dissatisfaction of ourselves,
Which at the same time, diminishes
Our sense of unity in the One....
The more we judge others,
The further we distance ourselves from the One!

When we feel "all right" with ourselves,
Judgment is seen to be very harmful....
The skeptic and scoffer,
Are now seen as manifestations...,
Of those who have judged too long,
Have sat for too long outside of the One, and pointed the finger!

Almost as if they had lived beyond their purpose,
As though they had existed past their prime,
Like fruit, rotting on the vine!

Chapter 5

 The Affliction

WOULD that I could wipe,
From the minds of men,
All feelings of inferiority,
Self-consciousness and guilt....

Those dreaded diseases...,
That separate one from another,
And shatter joy...,
Like glass....

Inferiority must be resolved in equality!
Self-consciousness dissolved in autonomy!
Guilt absolved in conformity to God's law!

One must be able to enter each moment free,
From the sense of guilt and inferiority,
In order to experience pure joy, unblemished,
As God would have us experience it!

Chapter 6

The Illusory Dream

WE slumber on the cusp of a new day,
One day we will wake up and find,
There will be no more fear, no ignorance....

No reason to hide behind half open doors, chained.
Glamour and vanity will dissipate with the morning dew.
There will be no more vices, crutches or quick suicides needed....

No sense of guilt or sin shall occupy your minds,
When the false teachings and teachers tumble and break upon the wave,
For having built their castles in the sand....

There will be no more greed or self gain,
All selfishness will cease as we begin to sow responsibly.
After all, your loss is not my gain, your fears, my shame....

Chapter 7

The Prodigal Path

TODAY, I have tasted of all the world's pleasure....
Though I am far from being complete, or even fulfilled,
Not to mention the bitter taste left in my mouth...,
At last, the lower man has died....

I have been merry, and drank the King's ale....
I have been glum, and drank peasant's rum....
I have searched far and wide for the elixir divine...,
But found instead, the Sorcerer's wine....

I have dug up the four corners of the earth...,
In hope to find jewels, and riches, and treasure chests!
But time and again, turned up only breasts...,
Bedecked in copper and tin of Nephilim's worth....

I have longed to close the circle of the embrace divine...,
Have two become one in union sublime...,
Yet even the sweetest ecstasy shared in time...,
Become memories divided..., yours and mine!

Chapter 8

The Lost Soul

TOO often, it is hard to assess,
Where we stand among the rocks and wood,
The lines that draw the path upon which we trod,
Become unclear, fuzzy, and indefinable....

All at once, standstill is mistaken for movement,
Forward is reversed, and wrong seems right.
Thank God for winds, and cosmic winds....
But today I shed tears of joy at a stranger's joy,

And I do feel sorrow when others suffer.
Am I then, too far from the mark?
At times, it is the heart alone that discerns a path,
The infallible compass that can only point true North!

Chapter 9

The Divine Conviction

AS I sit here calmly, without Christ...,
A revaluation of myself,
And all that I have created,
Becomes evident....

The old mold must be cast,
Upon the firm foundation of truth,
May all that is good, and pure, and of value,
Sit at the feet of the Lord, Christ....

And all that is impure,
And stagnate...,
Be scattered and recast,
By the breath of his spirit!

Chapter 10

The Laws of Life

ONE
EVERY thought that has a negative imprint
Will be eliminated by watchfulness!
TWO
EVERY word that has no positive imprint
Will be relinquished by thoughtfulness!
THREE
EVERY act that does not coincide with a pure conscience
Is strictly forbidden!
FOUR
ALL interactions will be conducted with love and understanding in mind!
FIVE
ALL interactions will be conducted with good intent and trust in mind!
SIX
ALL life emanates from "One Source" and will be treated with respect!
SEVEN
ALL life will depend on the "One Source" for all its needs!
EIGHT
ALL life will seek full integration with its "Source!"
NINE
ALL life will strive for full honesty always!
TEN
ALL life will be mindful of its "Source!"

Discrimination *is* the "Key!"
Christhood *is* the "Goal!"
Follow me....

Chapter 11

The Beat of Life

I AM unattached to the work of my hands,
Because I am not of the body!
I am attached to the work of my heart,
Because I am of the heart!

So reveals the silent watcher....
Heart is the abode of spirit...,
When spirit enters, the heart gives beat...,
When spirit departs, the heartbeat ceases....

Seek to know your heart, cleanse it and care for it.
For there will you find the "Prince of Peace,"
And the prize of your high calling,
It is the dwelling place of God!

Chapter 12

The Hum of Life

SACRED sound, come closer...,
As the tumult of the day dies,
I have sensed your presence,
Several times today,
Only to wander by!

So close, and yet so far...,
Do the day's activities keep you!
Though you never depart...,
You remain ever inviolate,
That naught can break apart!

Your ever present hum eludes me...,
As the roar of the world deludes me...,
Though the rising tide of the senses flood me...,
And the maddening world engulfs me...,
Your tone yet consoles me!

Chapter 13

The Mirror Image

MY soul,
A clear pool,
Of cool water!

Its surface,
Calmly mirrors,
Its surroundings....

Joy like a petal,
Carried on the winds,
Falls onto its surface...,

In expanding waves,
Of happiness,
Rippling through my flesh!

Chapter 14

The Base of Creation

IF you have ever underestimated the power of the "Father,"
Contemplate his all pervading presence and "Eternal Spirit,"
From which creation to creation unfolds....

If you have ever underestimated the power of the "Mother,"
Contemplate her magnificent manifold "Wombs of Matter,"
From which flows Homo sapiens to milky ways....

If you have ever underestimated the power of the "Son,"
Contemplate his divine incarnation as "The One, Across Time,"
From whom the gift of eternal life is conferred....

If you have ever underestimated the power of the "Holy Spirit,"
Contemplate her comfort dove and realm of "Hallowed Space,"
From which her advocacy is bestowed....

Chapter 15

The Creator's Clock

I DANCE on wheels turning,
From the hub of existence,
Juggling life and death,
Together endlessly....

Gathering experience,
And mastery as I go,
And a jolly good time,
Faster and faster they spin,

As I become older and wiser,
Most certainly a better balancer...,
I take in one culminating breath,
As the wheels of the cycle come to a halt,

I close my eyes...,
And swallow hard...,
And in a quantum moment,
I reset the clock!

Chapter 16

The Vine of Life

LILACS waft of incense fine,
An old man fills his pipe...,
Pine cones fall as squirrels dine,
A boat sits motionless adrift...,
The catfish leap upon the line.

Yelling children splash and shine,
The silence speaks louder still...,
Joking adults reflect prime,
As coyotes whine upon the hill,
Teens seek mysteries devoid of time.

The waves crash hard increasing tide,
A full moon waxes beyond the sill...,
Trees jest and gesture to cosmic chime,
As heaven creates a parents thrill...,
Souls ripen forth upon the vine!

Chapter 17

The Main Gate

BE assured there are a thousand and one paths of enchantment,
A thousand lifestyles, offering any possible realm of experience,
And a thousand more unimaginable!

Though in the end, each road or byway of this cosmic labyrinth,
Must eventually lead to the main gate, if we are going to advance,
Otherwise, we begin killing time, and accumulating karma....

No matter how far outward or inward we travel,
We must one day come to the door, upon which we must knock,
That door is the inner man of the heart, Christ....

But one must be made worthy in order to enter,
For no one goes to the Father except through the Son,
The Son is the mediator and guardian of the Father....

To knock upon this door, you must take yourself in hand,
And assume responsibility for yourself and your creation,
In the face of true reality, and Supreme Being!

Chapter 18

The Wedding Day

ONWARD, and upward,
My dear comrades,
These are old battles,
Only the wounds are new....

Look, even the enemy is exhausted,
Will you not finally,
Put an end to his misery?
He will thank you for it....

Besides there's an infinity,
Of victories ahead!
Can you not hear them calling?
We were not meant to dally here forever,

Each an Adam, an each an Eve....
Awake, and dress yourselves,
In the wedding garment!
Would you let your bridegroom wait?

Chapter 19

The Day of Rapture

THE "Day of Rapture" is at hand,
Awake all ye brides of Christ,
And claim your divine inheritance,
Prepare for the "Marriage of the Lamb!"

Make ready your temples,
And keep your lamps trimmed,
Adorn yourselves befitting,
And watch with vigilance!

And please do not mistake,
That I am speaking of the sleepers,
Nay, perhaps their night is not complete,
But to you my children, dear "Saints of Zion!"

Rejoice, and keep a song in your hearts,
The clouds of heaven are breaking apart,
Revealing the "Lion and his Legions,"
The remnant of Israel will soon depart!

Chapter 20

The Gift of Life

I AM Alpha, the Positive Polarity.
I am Omega, the Negative Polarity.
I am the Masculine Life Force.
I am the Feminine Life Force.
I am the Spiritual Flame of Identity.
I am the Material Form of Foundation.
We are "One!"

I am the Father.
I am the Mother.
I am the Will.
I am the Womb.
I am the Seed.
I am the Egg.
We are "One!"

I am I, the "One," the "Man Child!"
I am a "Focus" of the Will of the Father!
I am a "Locus" in the Womb of the Mother!
Drawn into the Womb of Matter...,
I am Spirit evolving in Time and Space!
I am the "Revealer" in the Creator's Parable!
I am the "Ancient Herald" come to bring you the "Word!"

I am the "Godchild," drawing warmth and nourishment through the bloodstream of Mother. Her life flowing into me, we are "One," cradled in the belly of her Cosmos...!

I know when she smiles..., I am content when she is calm..., and most secure when she loves..., I share her innermost thoughts..., an intimate union..., birth.... The "Gift of Life...."

CHAPTER 21

THE GIFT OF INNOCENCE

GOD'S children bring light and innocence,
The world to illumine...,
The people to enlighten...,
By nature they are uplifting,
God's gift to earth!

Guide God's children, in the way that they should go....
Teach them right by doing right, and to treat all as family....
Teach them kindness by being kind, with compassion to all....
Teach them cleanliness by being clean, in thought, speech, and deed,
And that the body is the temple of God!

Show them that the temple needs a keeper, by being a keeper....
Teach them that righteousness is the foundation...,
Upon which the temple is to be built...,
And that they are the builders....
Teach them that all men are responsible,

And held accountable for their selves before God...,
And that ignorance is no excuse for the Law....
Teach them truthfulness by being truthful...,
And that honesty is its own reward. Be quality Godparents,
So they will be quality Godchildren, and the earth be blessed!

Chapter 22

The Day of Initiation

LIGHT dawns upon me!
Illumination stirs within me!
A new revelation fills me!

I am done identifying with the body...,
For I am a sphere of eternal consciousness,
And consciousness is everything!

From this day forward...,
At the water's edge of the Pacific,
Some attainable goals emerge....

I will strive for new avenues of thought!
I will design new freeways of expression!
I will devise new highways of inspiration!
I will pave new roads to reason!

I will embody perfect thoughts and feelings!
I will exude perfect words and deeds!
I will remain perfectly seated in the "Eternal Now!"
The goddess of purity beckons..., and she is powerful!

CHAPTER 23

THE BAPTISM OF FIRE

I CAN feel it...,
The dormant one shakes,
She is rousing...,
The serpent awakes!

She makes me shudder,
The serpentine fire...,
With rolling thunder,
Ida and Pingala!

They begin the dance spiral,
As winged mercury...,
Ignites the caduceus,
With flames of purity!

And on up to its summit,
Where it seeks to enthrone...,
The thousand-petaled lotus,
As ecstasy unfolds!

Chapter 24

The Holy Communion

LIFE begins anew,
The Paraclete descends,
The goddess ascends,
They meet and join,
In Holy Communion!

And conceive the Christ child,
In the secret chamber of the heart!
Joy..., gratitude..., sanctified..., whole...,
Reborn in a baptism of fire...,
The higher path begins!

Chapter 25

The Hallowed Child

OH Magnificent blazing One,
To you do I owe eternal thanks!
By thy spirit, you breathe life,
Into form, Immaculate!
And bath it in radiant splendor!

Enfolding and in-firing thy creation with love by day,
And cooling it with the winds caresses by night,
Naught are you capable of but good,
Should man be content by doing less?
May thy corona be our testament to men!

Chapter 26

The Spiritual Mind

SITTING under a blissful sky, the rays of sunbeams shine upon me. The pounding surf begins to settle, the clamoring sound begins to cease. The third eye stabilizes the mind, allowing the inner vision to clarify and reflect the eternal, a sense of peace returns....

And what would the "Master Gardener" see on a day like this, what wonders would be revealed..., what thoughts would arise, and what perfection remains to be seen?

It is not only logical in the perfect sense, it is creatively brilliant. If one wishes a thing, plant the seed in mind and water it daily by thinking on it. If one wishes to be rid of a thing, pull up the weed and root, and forget about it completely, shutting it out of mind.

Every thought is a seed that will produce after its own kind. Be then the "Perfect Gardener" and thus nourish your souls, planting only the good and true sustaining fruits of virtue on your "Tree of Life," and all the while adding to the beauty and bounty of God's cosmic garden.

Oh yes, and when the waylaid and weary come to pick of your fruit, give them all that *you* can afford, but never more than *they* can use!

Chapter 27

The Carnal Mind

A DARK cloud of failure obscures my sun,
Though emerging from below...,
Such is the reward of the lower nature,
That severs the self from the source....

The last enemy, carnality...,
The derivative of one's sexual nature,
A product of my own making,
A sensual beast....

It is the nature of a man,
To need a woman to be complete!
It is the nature of a woman,
To need a man to be complete!

This bonding is the eternal flow,
Of the "Dyadic Embrace,"
It is the essential nature of each,
That completes the other....

Chapter 28

The Fall from Grace

SUDDENLY I stand face to face with my failure. An apparition of my human creation has come around full circle and is now an accumulating force and a formidable enemy. An enemy nourished by my habits of failure over time. You can be certain, there are many types of failure for the spiritually inclined, an action taken or not taken, a comment, a gesture, a look, a thought, a word spoken or unspoken, but none of these compare to the carnal, sin, temptation or vice, and each of these obstacles in turn, must be encountered, confronted, defeated, eliminated or mastered!

This force now intimidates me and prevents me from making any constant progress. It is my shadow self and it would dearly like to control me. It is the foe that bars entry into the higher planes of spiritual freedom. It is the "Dweller on the Threshold," the final adversary that must be overcome! It is the carnal mind. The sum total of my human miscreation, now become habit....

The great failures were built up by many smaller ones, of which I had convinced myself, were of no real threat, and unwittingly reinforced them into a great though negative force.... The proof of this being...,

"Failure & failure & failure = failure
And can *never* equal victory!"

And,

"Victory & victory & victory = victory
And can *never* equal failure!"

A reminder that the great victories are achieved by the accumulation of the everyday victories, the insignificant ones that eventuate into significant ones. In this wise, we gain a momentum of victory that will at one point literally carry us on to the ultimate victory!

CHAPTER 29

THE TEMPTATION

IF you are sincere in your spiritual aspirations, the need for continual right conduct and constancy cannot be stressed too highly, regardless of your required associations or environment. For what would it profit a man, if he conducted himself in a Saintly manner on the upward climb, but conducted himself in a Sinful manner on the downward slide? And how would it benefit a soul, whose desire is to ascend the mountain of God, that one might avail himself of the "Grace of God," yet continually stumbled and fell, succumbing to sin, temptation or desire?

The answer is straightforward, you would get nowhere fast, and that is the reward of failure, inconstancy, the falling prey to temptation, of an unexamined flaw or weakness of character, regardless of the form the failure takes....

Then, there is only one alternative, you must pick yourself up from your bootstraps, and begin again....

Inconstancy *is* a flaw on the first or tenth step!
Weakness *will not* change of its own accord!
Failure *will* follow you as far as you let it!
Temptation *cannot* be avoided, but overcome and mastered!

These are the ultimate tests of your will to prevail in your spiritual quests. And for this reason they will follow you to the very gates of heaven.

At long last, we know the fate of a "Star" that grows inconstant, and the destiny of a "Sun" that conducts itself accordingly....

In regard to the soul, right conduct equals constancy, which equals immortality, for immortality is a constant!

Chapter 30

The Crossroads of Life

THE sum of one's being is equivalent to the sum of one's decisions. With each decision we make, regardless of how seemingly unimportant it may be we are confronted with a fork in the road, not to the right or to the left, but upward or downward....

Each moment we live we are faced with decisions. Today's decisions determine tomorrow's karmic creation. May they free you and not fetter you....

Indecision *is* a decision.... Its *price* makes you the victim of circumstance!
Inactivity *is* a decision.... Its *price* is prolongation and lost opportunity!
Inconstancy *is* a decision.... Its *price* is failure and instability!

Each decision we make allows us the opportunity to progress or regress. Each progression takes us up to the next step on the spiral staircase. Each regression takes us down to the next step.

Decisions are now seen as investments in ourselves. Each wise decision enriches us, and brings us closer to our destination. Each foolish one delays our journey, but allows us the opportunity to learn from our mistakes. If we refuse to learn, we begin to impoverish ourselves.

This is the crux of the matter. We were given seed, talents and consciousness so that we could put them to wise use, and multiply them, for the Creator's pleasure. Therefore, impoverishing and wasting the gifts we have been given is an offense to the Creator.

The complexities involved in attaining self-perfection, can be reduced to its lowest denominator..., decision. Self-mastery is the result of correct decisions.

May you ponder the consequences of your decisions beforehand! Your life depends on them!

Chapter 31

The Coin of the Realm

OBEDIENCE to the "Will of God" and to His precepts is the "Coin of the Realm" for the earnest aspirant on the spiritual path. But who can ascend the mountain of God, and who can withstand the presence of God? Only those with clean hands and a clean heart!

Prepare yourselves disciples, and mind your hearts and hands, oh aspirants, seekers, wayfaring men and women of all lands and seas, for this is your prerequisite!

But for this you must be tested and tried by the "Flaming Hand" of God Himself, so that you may be found worthy, ready, and acceptable in His sight. It is the kindness of God that prohibits the unworthy, and the unready an audience with Him, for by virtue of the very composition of His "Being," He is too pure to behold iniquity, and darkness is consumed in His presence, thus, the unworthy, the unready, and the unacceptable would perish before Him, like a moth before a flame. Only a flame can abide a flame!

Thus, as we follow and obey the "Will of God," His "Code of Life" and His "Manifold Laws and Precepts," we begin to enter into a "New Life" based on spiritual principle, understanding and harmony which is the basis of "Life" itself.

The alchemy that occurs as we live in understanding and loving obedience to the "Divine Source" will eventually transform the "Coin of the Realm" into the "Key of the Realm," that will unlock the door to cosmic being, knowledge, reality and privilege. And will provide you, the righteous and solitary wanderer with the long awaited and well deserved liberation from the seemingly endless cycles of "Samsara" or rebirth. Which from this point on, goes hand in hand with cosmic responsibility, for a "Grand and Mystical Knowledge" requires and equally "Grand Responsibility," one the new adept and worker in white magic is well equipped to face!

CHAPTER 32

THE ROD OF OBEDIENCE

THE "Charge of God's Will,"
Must be "Grounded" in obedience....

Obedience is the rod,
God uses to temper and test us....

The obedient beast is spared the rod...,
The mindful monk is spared the reprimand....

Of this, we have no option.
Or, it is no idle threat...,

You will be jolted back,
Into harsh reality!

Chapter 33

The Key to Reparation

IF you seek to know God's will, consider this,
God's will is always in accordance with man!
The beginning of difficulty arises,
When man's will,
Ceases to be congruent with God's....

You must first begin by closing the circle,
An understanding of natural law,
Will enable you to sense the flow of the Tao,
Sensing how Tao flows is the first step,
In letting go....

The current of God's will,
Naturally flows through Tao!
There is no other current....
To enter one stream is to enter the other,
Thus closing the gap!

Chapter 34

The Realization of Truth

BE assured that the path of truth will eventually bring you to the point, where you will know perfectly well through harvested experience, preceded by many a failed crop, that the words of Christmas Humphreys ring true, and could not have been expressed better. He says...,

"We are punished *by* our sins, not *for* them."

Will one day cause you to cry out in the realization that all is just, and all is fair! That in truth, there is no divine injustice, rather the wrong use of man's freewill. But by this time you will be working with the Tao!

Chapter 35

The Key to Harmony

THE key to successful work is order!
Order is the movement of grace....
Grace is the flow of the Tao....
The Tao is God flowing into us....
The key to orderliness however, is God!

The key to successful living is harmony!
Harmony is the movement of order....
Order is the flow of the Tao....
The Tao is God flowing into us....
The key to harmony however, is God!

CHAPTER 36

THE MEASURE OF A MAN

GOD, everything manifest is God....
God is the "Foundation Stone" and grid of creation....
Man is the "Manifested Grid" in the process of becoming....
Tao is the "Universal Medium" and flow of creation....

God creates everything by means of Tao....
God grows the plant "Man" by means of Tao....
God harvests everything by the means of Tao and Man....
God designs, builds and creates by the means of Tao and Man....

Men design furnishings to accommodate God's form....
Men build fixtures to assist God's needs....
Men create manuscripts to express God's thoughts....
All is created by God by the means of Tao and Man....

God is the "Immortal Grid" of creation! Tao is the "Medium" of creation!
Man is the "Mortal Grid" in the process of becoming!
So I ask you, what is the measure of a man...,
If everything manifest is God?

Chapter 37

The Considerate

TIME and again they protest saying,
Not harmlessness but helpfulness,
Will unlock the door to the kingdom of heaven!

But I insist that, harmlessness,
Is the epitome of helpfulness,
In its broadest sense!

Whether you help your brother in need,
Or truly cause him no harm...,
The end justifies the means!

Chapter 38

The Divine Immunity

HARMLESSNESS and fearlessness go hand in hand!
The greater the harmlessness of an individual,
The less fear he is subject to..., which can be proven in this way,
Anyone who hurts life, no matter the magnitude, hurts God.
Whoever hurts life has a valid reason to fear, life's retribution....

While those who consciously help life by manifesting,
Harmlessness in thought, speech and deed,
In essence assist God, and thereby experience,
A corresponding sense of protection and fearlessness...,
In the midst of an awesome and respected Cosmos!

Chapter 39

The Grace of God

BE not deceived...,
There is an "Eternal Will,"
Flowing through us...,
Expressing it through us...,
Impressing it through us...,
Perfecting it through us...,
Indeed, living through us....

From nucleonic spark, onward!
Raising us to His high ideal, the "Anointed One,"
By His immaculate, benevolent will.
One must enter the river of that "Will," and let go...,
The current taking you where it will, though all rivers that live,
Flow to the sea of "Original Source," like the rain returns to the river,
The "Eternal Will of Perfection" returns us until perfected!

Chapter 40

The Whited Sepulchers

MY last four consecutive jobs,
I've worked with corpses...,
Vacuums..., posing as ordinary people,
Not an easy task to keep joyful,
They rape you thoroughly..., but....

The toil of the workplace...,
Has now become the tilling of the fields!
Our sowing and reaping...,
Has now become our wheat and chaff!
The time of harvest is at hand....

CHAPTER 41

THE TEMPLES OF RUIN

DO you believe in haunted houses my friend?
Do you believe in houses inhabited by the spirit?
Do you believe that the body is the temple of God?
And the dwelling place of his spirit?
Then it follows....

When the spirit of God departs the vessel,
The temple is denuded of life!
As nature abhors a vacuum...,
Everything unlike God pours in to fill the void,
Emotions, desire, moods and entities....

Astral effluvia unreal and impure,
Begins to animate and manipulate...,
Until the body is no longer your own!
Do you believe in haunted houses my friend?
Do you believe in haunted souls?

Chapter 42

The Valley of Bones

DEATH and hell are nipping at my heels,
Would that it were only my heels....
I see its pallid face everywhere,
Its arid scent sucks the moisture from the air....

Bodies with no essence sit where I sit,
People I would not..., want to touch me,
Everyone talks about..., nothing,
And they expect an answer!

Chapter 43

The Living and the Dead

SO the earth is host to the living and the dead...,
Mother is impartial, yet the dead surround us....
God's light shines upon the just and the unjust,
The living and the dead impersonally....

The living are sustained and nourished!
The dead are scorched and made hollow!
The living reed sways and conforms to the wind of the spirit!
But the dead reed snaps and is blown upon the winds....

Chapter 44

🌾 The Voice in the Wilderness 🌾

THERE was a man they say, recently found running,
Into the silent woods frantic..., some say he was a madman,
A sorry chap, a blemish on society, an outcast....

His cries echoed from the wilderness in search of God,
Looking under stone and brush, and whatever else could be lifted,
He would sprint from trunk to trunk, and listen for the voice of God...,
Nothing!

Sweating up hill and down dale for long hours he would cover terrain,
Then sink half hidden behind a log, hoping that God might stumble along,
Alone and dejected he sobbed, darkness at length obscured his sight...,
Nothing!

There was a man they say, lately found running,
To and fro the forest panting..., some say he was a prophet, a saint,
Sent to show men the way, who suffocated in the wasteland!

Chapter 45

 The Barren Fields

IN regard to man,

A consciousness, seed or talent that has neither multiplied nor become fruitful! A barren field or soul that has become impoverished and can no longer sustain life!

One in which their "talents" and "gifts" have been allowed to remain dormant. Some of which their "seeds" and "abilities" have been allowed to dissipate and be lost. Others of which their "values" and "consciousnesses" have degenerated into vice, addiction and avarice!

Those who have not been responsible tillers of their fields, and have let their rich fertile "lands" and "endowments" dwindle into dry and lifeless estates. Those whose virtues offer no fruit or nourishment to a weary traveler, and whose vines have become withered.

Those who have forgotten the "One" who had bestowed their original talents and charged them to sow responsibly, and so have cut themselves off from the parent vine. Those whose values are no longer attuned to the wisdom of the eternal!

The wasteland contains many who have settled down to nest on the perch called "happiness through pleasure." A comfortable nest where there is no real struggle, until the earth quakes.

The event that these domesticated virtues, seeds and talents could again become fruitful and multiply is indeed possible, but there is only one way. There is only "One Source" for salvation! Only God can transform the withered limb into one flowing with life....

Meanwhile, the wasteland bakes!

Chapter 46

The False Virtues

EVERYWHERE I go I meet the good people. Well conformed ones. They are nice and smile occasionally. They stand well in lines and seldom get out of line. They follow all the conventions of the world, and take the world's advice on how to live their lives....

They wait for all the bargains at the stores, to waste their money on more useless things. They often eat out, and let their appetites determine what fills their stomachs, instead of wisely choosing nutrition. They leave modest tips at restaurants if they like you, or decide they don't like you in order to leave none....

Many slog through the nine to five to get wasted on the weekend. Others "relax" in front of their televisions, hydrating themselves with alcohol, cursing their winning teams when they lose. Still others plant themselves in front of that unblinking eye, trancelike, feeding the Beast from morning 'til night....

You may find some of them in church on Sunday, who will offer you all kinds of assistance, until you really need it. They will offer to give you the shirts off their backs, but expect you to repay the loan. They will praise you in private and curse you in public. Even offer to share their homes with you, if they are sure you don't need it.

You will find many of them on the Sabbath, faithfully buying their lottery tickets at the corner liquor stores. The fearless ones spend their mornings at church, and their afternoons at their favorite casinos....

They fear the police, but mostly the neighbors, and keep their doors locked. They are comfortably civilized people, but their modest goodness and conforming nature is of a degenerate kind. It is not life in the ascendancy but rather life in a crevice or nook of stagnation. Life itself has simmered down to a miserable ease. There is no longer a spiritual impetus in their lives. The spirit of God..., all but departed.

Their harmlessness and beliefs have not redeemed them, nor will they.... Enough of the worldly values of good and just! May purity of heart and mind be the gold of our attainment!

Chapter 47

The False Values

THIS is not to say that pleasure is a bad thing. Moderation to be sure is the key to all happiness! It is only to say that the "values" of pleasure and happiness will never lead you to perfection in and of themselves.

This being the case, they should be seen for what they are, decoys that lure you away from the path of knowledge and self discovery, objects of enticement in which one day you'll grow weary, but only after much wasted time and disappointment.

Look today, at the reigning values of the 21st. Century man, look at the mindsets, look at the get something for nothing mentality, look at the play to win mentality, look at the hit the lottery or jackpot mentality, look at the become a millionaire mentality, and all of these mentalities and mindsets desirous of great wealth, pleasure, ease, rest and luxury without having toiled for them, sweat for them, worked for them, or earned them.

True wealth, pleasure, ease, rest and luxury are the just rewards of the honest, hard working man or woman who have sweat for them, have worked hard for them, and have earned them! Only then are the "values" of pleasure and happiness justified. Even the Creator will not deny the hard working man or woman the fruits of their labor.

In six days God created the heaven and the earth, and all that therein is, and on the seventh day he rested!

The un-talked about "values" of pleasure and happiness must be exposed, talked about and renounced as the reigning values. A correct sense of values must be reinstituted based on the principles of work, accomplishment and earning, which in turn provide a correct sense of proportion and supply to the receiver, which in turn restores the spiritual to physical relationship.

Then, all is well, the spiritual values become the reigning "values" and you become the living manifestation of them. They must become the true primary values, from which all else flows. Then great wealth is in the hands of great wisdom, and all is good under heaven. One day you will realize this. Then and only then will true joy and happiness return to you!

Chapter 48

The Pure Advantage

IT is not the rich, the well-connected,
Or the powerful that are the privileged few,
But rather the pure and wise who harbor few desires...,
I have seen it a thousand times....

The angry or the rude never get the service they desire,
And often have to return to the end of the line....
While the kind and gentle get better service than they desire...,
Often with no line at all!

The impure struggle to achieve their ends,
And sense invisible doors close before them....
The pure not focused on themselves achieve their ends...,
And sense invisible mountains move before them....

The hurried are detained!
The at-ease sustained!
The pure are the truly privileged!
Status or wealth, have nothing to do with it!

Chapter 49

The Absolution of Sin

HOW does one become pure in an impure world? It is important to remember that we were once pure. Since man's fall from grace in Eden, mankind has continually lowered the level of purity, and increased the level of iniquity in the world to its present state by its habitual patterns of imperfect thinking which have inevitably resulted in its imperfect deeds, ad infinitum....

The habits of wrong thinking and doing must be broken. The old molds must be recast into new molds so that a new regenerate man and woman can come about. God will not put new wine into old wineskins, for it would negatively affect the new wine...

First
We have to acknowledge *our* fall from grace from the beginning!

Second
We have to understand that *we* were born into sin and that *we*
Remain that way until *we* seek redemption from God!

Third
We must repent of *our* sins and renounce evil!

Finally
We must invite Christ into *our* lives to be *our* Savior and Salvation!

In this way, we absolve our creation, and pass from death unto life. We become renewed, reborn and transfigured wineskins, prepared to receive the new wine. The "Grace of God" is the new wine and a new man and woman will surely result!

Chapter 50

The Pure Genius

THE condition or manifestation of genius originates at the atomic level and is directly dependent upon the quality of purity inherent within the four lower bodies or elements of man. Since the four lower vehicles of man are comprised of the four elements of nature, purity affects and improves the physiology of man....

Genius *is* therefore a matter of physiology and purity!

This being the case, that the wisest men throughout the ages have been the purest? The question of whether or not genius is dependent upon hereditary factors is not putting the question right. Undoubtedly, many genetic characteristics are passed on from parents, but on matters of genius, what is critical and hereditary is the quality of purity of the seed of the Father, combined with the quality of purity of the egg of the Mother, that will determine the brilliance of the child....

Purity *is* brilliance!

However, the seed of the male and the egg of the female cannot be purer than the whole of each one. This is why the fruit does not fall too far from the tree, or parent! The law of nature prescribes that seeds produce after their kind. This law applies to man as well. The impure seed of a man cannot bring forth a pure child, but rather a relatively similar one, just as the pure seed cannot bring forth an impure one.
Once purity has been vouchsafed to the incoming child, the complimentary factors of upbringing, proper nutrition, environment and education will produce the brilliant offspring or offshoot of the parents.
The manifestation of genius does not depend solely on the level of intelligence of a man.... It depends equally upon the level of purity of a man, which in turn determines the potential for intelligence!

Chapter 51

The Moderate Man

MODERATION and preservation,
Go hand in hand...,
Which, can be proven in this way,

Too much of a good thing,
Ceases to be a good thing...,
And soon becomes its opposite!

Alas, the immoderate man,
Through lack of control,
Is consumed by his appetites!

Reason enough to avoid excess,
And how every good thing is preserved...,
Through moderation!

Chapter 52

The Eternal Treasure

THE worldly man's treasure,
Held in his unnatural mind...,
Consists of trinkets and gold,
Jewelry, coin and paper...,
Stored in banks and vaults...,
That can be lost or taken from him!

While the spiritual man's treasure,
Held in his natural mind...,
Lay secure in eternal truths,
And nuggets of knowledge,
Stored in heart and mind...,
That can never be taken from him!

Chapter 53

The Will of Man

ALTHOUGH it is true that all beings are grounded in the infinite, it is not usually true that they are properly aligned with their infinite source. True alignment with "One's Source" guarantees that one is square rooted or square built in regard to one's existence. This in turn guarantees success in all aspirations and endeavors undertaken by the individual.

Being correctly aligned or rooted with "One's Source" allows us the ability to make solid judgments and correct decisions. It is now seen as the prerequisite of proper building. This is why the house built on the rock will remain, while the house built on the shifting sands will crumble....

However, in order to achieve true alignment, one must hold nothing back from that infinite source and be completely honest in all respects. Any dishonesty will exclude you from complete union or "Oneness" with the source because righteous living is all honesty and truth and goodness. It is the right use or utilization of God's grace flowing into you and through you that makes you righteous.

If the being of man can be likened to a tree destined to bear fruit and multiply, the need to be properly aligned and firmly planted is essential if one is to grow up well!

Chapter 54

The Will of God

GOETHE'S proposition that "the eternal womanly draws us upward" sounds wonderful, albeit, somewhat vague. I propose that "the eternally perfect draws us to perfection" is more to the point, thus closer to the truth....

God is the "absolute magnet" which draws that portion of the eternal will in us, back to the source of the "Eternal Will." God is also absolute perfection in which no amount of relative perfection could abide. Hence, if we are ultimately destined to return to God from whence we came, the requirement of perfecting that portion of the eternal will in us becomes of paramount importance.

Re-embodiment is the natural means of fulfilling the spiritual "Law of Perfection." Everyone must return until perfected and without an eternal will or spirit working through us there would be no return. Without an eternal will or spirit there would be only nothingness....

The event that man, consisting of such magnificent things as mind and matter, spirit and soul, could attain the state of spiritual perfection in the span of a mere lifetime is a ridiculous notion.

If time were erased and forgotten, the span of a lifetime would be an instant in eternity. The thought of becoming perfected in that instant is totally unrealistic and an affront to the Creator.

Time and space are facades, all that exists are absolutes. Relative acts of good and evil eventually decay and dissolve for they are "in reality" non-existent.

It is not the Creator's fault that you relate to the world of appearances, or that you interpret your lives according to those appearances. The only relatives that exist are the erroneous interpretations of your world!

CHAPTER 55

 THE FINITE MIND

PARACELSUS wrote,

"Philosophy *is* only the true perception and
Understanding of cause and effect...."

We can't argue against such logic and must ultimately accept it as true. I would further add the fact, that "true perception and understanding is possible only when the mind of the perceiver is clean, free and unfettered."

William Blake said,

"If the doors of perception were cleansed,
Everything would appear to man as it *is*, infinite!"

A clean mind is essential in that it is a mirror capable of reflecting reality. Therefore, the perceptions and interpretations of the philosopher may be as clear or distorted as the mind permits, wholly dependent upon the condition of the instrument itself....

I would further like to add that "one must be pure and enlightened in order to interpret pure reality," let alone cause and effect. Each mental state perceives reality differently until they become pure! The pure in heart and mind all interpret reality similarly, hence the "Oneness" of the Logos!

CHAPTER 56

THE INFINITE MIND

DALI did to the world of art, what others tried so hard to repress. Namely, he stood it on its head, by bringing all the seething undercurrents of the unconscious mind to the surface, to the threshold of perception.

But the obvious question remains, of what "value" is there in exposing such things, except to bring as proof to the greater awareness of people that we all possess an unconscious portion of mind. That it is an unfathomable pool wherein coherency and logic do not apply. That in fact, underneath our conscious minds is a boundless field without means of measure, and that what cannot be measured, cannot be known.

This boundless field is the abyss, where ultimately, one is tried and tested. It is the crucible where character is found, it is the furnace where one's metal is tested. It is the place where the eternal man will finally emerge. It is likewise, the place where the weak-minded, the corrupt, and the faint-hearted are purged, that's right, all within the parameters of your own mind....

It is the ultimate frontier. The unconscious portion of mind is like space that cannot be fully explored or comprehended. Hence, it is beyond any fixed interpretation of knowledge.

This leaves us with the original observation... that the larger portion of existence and mind are still in the realm of question and obscurity!

As there is only "One Mind" in the universal grid, it remains the supernal unknown!

Chapter 57

The Spiral Staircase

THE pole of consciousness runs vertically coiled about by steps or stages that run clockwise as we ascend and counter-clockwise as we descend. Each acquisition of divine knowledge along with its mastery and correct assimilation allows us the opportunity to step up onto the next rung of the ladder.

Since divine knowledge can never be exhausted, the raising of one's consciousness never ends. The potential for your expansion into God's consciousness is everlasting and equally open to all.

The states of consciousness that we refer to as heaven and hell are but opposite ends of the pole. It is the state of purity of any given life-stream that determines the plane and environment in which a person will find one self upon incarnating. That degree of purity in turn establishes the vibratory pattern of the individual. Every sentient life form exudes a tone. It is the pulsation of this tone that makes up the vibratory pattern of the overall life.

As consciousness *is* everything, the purification of consciousness purifies the overall life. As the consciousness of a life-stream becomes purer, the external environment will change accordingly and shift up to its proper plane of expression, therefore...,

---

A clean mind *will* be born into a clean environment!
A sullied mind *will* be born into a sullied environment!

This is why God's consciousness can never be contaminated. It is so extremely high above the minds of men due to its absolute purity and vibration.

This is also where knowledge can be your best friend or worst enemy. With each increase of spiritual knowledge, one must correspondingly raise the degree of purity within one's being in order to continue advancing on the right-handed path. For to strive for eternal knowledge while neglecting the precepts of right living, right conduct and right thinking, will surely lead you down the left-handed path. For black magic is a desecration of God's alchemy because the doer is impure!

Divine knowledge is the key in which to attain more of God, but purity is the door to the higher octaves of God awareness and God reality. If you want to experience more of God, you must become more like him. Such wonderful safeguards has the Almighty established that no one can change, hence, the "Divine Immutability of the Law of the One."

Thus, heaven and hell are inextricably tied to consciousness, but as has previously been said, consciousness *is* everything! Thus, they are as real as your own reality. When we read such works as the "*Holy Bible,*" or "*The Dhammapada*" of the Buddha Gotama, or Dante's "*Divine Comedy,*" the differing extremes of experience demonstrate where they were positioned along the pole of consciousness during that particular embodiment or stage of their soul's life.

When we read their writings, we are not only experiencing their sojourns in time and space, we are experiencing their states of consciousness that are added to our own. As all knowledge is retained at the soul level it will remain there until accessed for our benefit....

Hence,

> The "Imagery" of the Bible's New Jerusalem...,
> *Becomes* your image of heaven!
>
> The "Imagery" of the Buddha's nirvana...,
> *Becomes* your image of bliss!
>
> The "Imagery" of Dante's hell...,
> *Becomes* your image of hell!

It is not unusual for the soul to remain at any given stage of experience and understanding for several incarnations. Each person can and does ascend and descend the pole of consciousness numerous times as experience warrants to dwell in planes of bliss or of damnation according to their karmic creation.

Taking into account that an evildoer cannot enter into the consciousness of heaven, may be reason enough to refer to this pole as the pole of perfection also!

Chapter 58

The Positive and Negative

THE pole of consciousness is also a magnetic pole. The positive polarity pulls us upward throughout eternity. The negative pole pulls us downward. The heart of man is the crucible where plus and minus struggle for supremacy throughout the ages, as the soul is being developed, eventually the soul comes to understand the polarities of its own nature, whereby they can finally be reconciled and balanced. Only then can the soul achieve true rest from the incessant warring of its dual nature.

The heart of man is the equator that divides the higher nature from the lower nature. God, the absolute magnet draws us upward to perfection and integration, made the master of our pure desire. Carnality, the relative magnet draws us downward to destruction and disintegration, made the slave of our impure desire.

An example of consciousness having a magnetic pull should become obvious to you if you are honest and observe your patterns of habit and vice. When one is not in control of one's mind, it becomes idle, and soon begins to gravitate toward a dominant habit, or pleasure....

All habits exert a magnetic pull on the mind. The intensity of the pull is determined by the length of the habit and the frequency of occurrence. They become so strong that if not satiated, they can cause irritability and anger, hence the repetitive destructive nature of habit.

This is not to be taken lightly. Powerful patterns of habit are carried over from lifetime to lifetime if not disassembled and broken. They not only keep us bound to their vibratory band on the lower planes, they keep us bound at a certain level of consciousness on that plane, a plane shared by others of similar consciousness....

That means,

>The addict *shares* a plane with the addict....
>The fearful *share* a plane with the fearful....
>The unbeliever *shares* a plane with the unbeliever....
>The abominable *share* a plane with the abominable....
>The murderer *shares* a plane with the murderer....

And so on, and so forth....

Hence, the injunction to look at yourselves in an honest fashion, determine which habits and impediments are keeping you down so that they can finally be disassembled and removed from your lives.

Arise, sons and daughters of God, free yourselves from bondage, break those chains and shackles, vanquish all vice, rise to your rightful place and claim your divine inheritance.... For the Lord is come to "Judge the Earth!" The "Day of Liberation" is at hand!

Chapter 59

The Burden of Density

AS above, so below...,

The main difference between God and his progeny is manifold, but primarily one of magnitude, and subsequently, one of location. The greater the magnitude of spirit, the lesser the weight of density, the lighter the molecular weight, the lesser the "Law of Gravity" applies....

The proof of this being,

The "Ascension" of Christ himself, after having transmuted every vestige of human density and desire, he became one of increasing spiritual magnitude. So buoyant that the physical "Law of Gravity" could no longer contain him, and so he ascended to the plane of spirit.
The spiritually liberated soul is able to choose his location from among the Father's many mansions....

Physical laws are *relative* to time and space!
Spiritual laws are *absolute* within the universal grid!

Newton said, "What goes up must come down." Observe the relativity of this law in relation to the "Law of Ascension." "What descends must also ascend," but that is a matter of time and wisdom!

Chapter 60

The Planes of Desire

CRIPPLES occupy a plane!
Paranoiacs occupy a plane!
Drug addicts occupy a plane!
Criminals occupy a plane!
Neurotics occupy a plane!
Mechanized man, are likewise bound to a plane!

One of the most illuminating statements in all of psychology was uttered by Sigmund Freud, he said...,

"The neurotic *repeats*, instead of *remembering*."

Oh, what wonderful changes could be wrought if "Man" would only remember the errors of his ways? It is not that man does not remember, he remembers full well, it is only that his neurosis has re-wired his thought processes to bypass the undesired remembrance. At first, it was a matter of remembering, that was discarded over time because the action was more desirable than the remembrance. Over time, the action of not remembering became habit, and the resultant thought processes became hard wired into their being.

When "Man" refuses to learn the lessons of failure over time, that are conducive to change, the Lord God turns them over to a reprobate mind, and then they truly enter the miasma of the clouded mind, with veiled understanding. They become creatures with confusion of face, and of separate existence, the affliction ensues, the neurosis continues, ad infinitum!

"*Remember* brothers and sisters, and *you* would do well!"

Mechanized man, are humans devoid of God. The ones in which Jesus rebuked saying, "you do not enter into heaven yourselves, and you keep those who are entering from entering."

When Jesus said, "no man is crippled, except in his soul." He was pointing out the fact that the souls of men can be lame, even as the physical form manifests that lameness. If a man is born lame, then that man upon maturation should search his soul for the true cause of the affliction, so that it can be corrected. In this way, the next round of re-embodiment will be whole and good, the cause of the affliction eliminated, so that the spiritual path can begin.

I am not referring to the innocent lives that become maimed or disabled because they are put in harm's way. Acts of war, the accidents of life, the victims of illness and atrocity prove the cruelty of the world we live in, and the cruel nature of men. These souls are not lame. They are the true "martyrs" who have taken the sins of the world upon themselves, in the true fashion of the Christ. They are the ones heading toward the "New Jerusalem."

It is certain now that there are as many planes as there are vibratory rates of purity, which vary in degree infinitesimally. These planes interpenetrate each other ever so subtly, as the lower vehicles of man become less pure, the density of his world will increase, which in turn determine his external surroundings, his hardships and obstacles, his opportunities or lack thereof.

This is why moving from city to city, or job to job, or mate to mate, will not permanently improve your condition. If you want to lastingly improve your life and your environment, you must do it by changing your ways and patterns of living, and your associations if necessary. You must develop new habits and regenerate ways of thinking that foster a righteous life, and find new recreations that are congruent with a clean conscience.

So the surrounding environment corresponds completely to the "Desire" and quality of "Cleanliness" within the heart, which at the same time adjusts the level of purity within the temple of man!

THE SCALES OF JUSTICE

THAT an act of kindness or unkindness will return to us at a later date to help or hinder us in our endeavors may be easily refuted, unless we understand "Karma" as consisting of essentially energy, and furthermore, as energy returning to us to be balanced or utilized correctly....

When God established the "Law of Freewill," he also implemented the "Law of Karma" so that man's personal use of energy could be monitored in accordance with his "Works," so that the "Law of Justice" and "Law of Opportunity" could be unerringly maintained.

As man began to experiment with the use and abuse of freewill, he unwittingly got himself caught up in the web of cause and effect. By dabbling in the fields of relative good and evil, he became fully absorbed in the world of appearances and is now functioning in the realm of "Maya." A myopic state where one can no longer see the forest for the trees. "Maya" is the illusory dream state where appearance takes precedent over the "Unified Whole," which is the underlying grid or network of life.

When things become things in themselves, the origin of creation is lost. A mere imitation of life results, the dream of "Maya" ensues and ones separate existence from "Source" begins.

It has been rightly said that "God is absolutely just and that the universe is absolutely just," therefore, all injustice or seeming injustice stems from the human miscreation, the misqualification of God's grace, man's freewill.

In this light, it is seen that the "Law of Karma" is inextricably woven into the "Law of Justice" as a tool of learning. That, as a matter of fact, reward and punishment are not executed by the Godhead, but rather, we reward or punish ourselves under "Divine Law!"

CHAPTER 62

The Waves of Karma

TO each his own karma,
From first incarnation,
To the last,
Multiplied by millions....

May give you some sort of an idea,
As to what tremendous forces must manifest,
On a national level in order to restore,
Justice, balance, and equilibrium....

Although the sum aggregate,
Of a nation's karma,
Is that of its combined citizens!
It may be dealt out on a national level,

So that greater quantities of equilibrium,
May be restored more rapidly...,
Does not alter the fact that individual karma,
Ceaselessly returns to its maker!

Chapter 63

THE CRUCIBLE OF TIME

MANKIND chase externals,
Race to the void...,
Symbol of its lack of internal grace,
Reflects condition of mind,
More of its age....

The young mind seeks externals!
The mature mind seeks internals!
The young heart seeks appearances!
The mature heart seeks essences!

Is mankind then...,
A complacent elder,
Or naïve adolescent,
Let's hope youth is the answer...,
Adulthood at stake!

Chapter 64

The Inexperienced Man

THERE was an innocent man who belonged to an indigenous tribe of warriors in the tropical rain forest. His daily tasks consisted mainly of hunting and gathering food for his clan. When the need for food was secured, he would make weapons and tend to the needs of his village. The man lived, ate and slept in a natural spontaneous way. He hunted and killed when he was hungry, he slept when the sun set, and procreated upon the cyclic urge to procreate.

For the tribesmen, the concepts of planning for their futures or to have children are non-existent, they just happen. Once their immediate needs are met, they pass their time in recreation, storytelling and devising crafts. Ceremonies arise accompanied by instinctual music and dance. They are not concerned with tomorrow and are not bound by the past. They live solely in the present moment, much like the Zen masters of the Orient, but that is where the similarity ends....

The true Zen master is extremely conscious of his relationship with the universe, time and space, and with the nature of the Tao. The master of Zen knows who he is, and why he is what he is.

The tribesman in truth does not know who he is, and therefore, does not know why he is what he is. It is simply not an option from his realm of experience. It is the difference between an experienced man and an inexperienced man.

The odd part of the tale begins when one of the tribesmen was arrested for killing an animal outside the boundary of his village's hunting ground. He was apprehended and put in jail by an official and was given no explanation as to his unfortunate predicament.

The otherwise healthy tribesman died within a week of his being detained. A doctor was brought in to ascertain the cause of death, but to his befuddlement, no cause of death could be determined. It was of the doctor's opinion that the man had simply chosen to stop living....

The tribesman lost the will to live! And the relationship between "freedom and movement" had everything to do with it. To have separated him from the earth and the wind and the "freedom of movement" was evidently a separation from life itself.

Unable to conceptualize being released in the future, he was confronted with a bleak inhospitable present. Incapable of coping mentally with the enormity of his situation, left him only the will to die.

Proof..., that a healthy will can choose to live, or choose to die. In contrast, look today at the separate, unhealthy multitudes where the will to acquiring..., consumerism..., escapism..., idleness..., pleasure, without having earned it..., or just surviving are the norms, their determining values.

It is not unusual today to see millions devoid of the will to live, yet without sufficient will left to die!

CHAPTER 65

THE EXPERIENCED MAN

THE will of Zen is at once spontaneous, natural and attuned with its environment, unencumbered with personal hang-ups and psychological complexes so abundant in the West today.

Disorders such as introversion, depression, anxiety, compulsions and obsessions so prevalent in modern America are brought on no doubt by a separatist way of living. A separation primarily from one's source, and subsequently from nature, and ultimately from one's own self or mind.

These separations make it impossible to achieve any lasting success or true happiness in life, or in any endeavor one undertakes, and is precisely the reason why they are sternly frowned upon by the Zen master. The Zen master understands the relationship between "Cause and Effect," and therefore acknowledges one's separation from one's source as the cause of the real affliction, and not the disorder. Thus, they do not put the cart before the horse.

A master of Zen is a master of the elements. To understand the foundation from which he operates, you might as well contemplate the clouds in the sky, or the sound of the rustling wind through the trees, or the raindrops of spring pummeling a pond. He is at once attuned to the formed and the unformed, the seen and the unseen, and although he can be harsh or stern, "because nature is sometimes harsh or stern," it is in an impersonal sense, much like nature.

The Zen master's quality of "Oneness" is his source of confidence and security even in the midst of uncertainty. There is no place for fear in a person who knows his self to be the center of the universe. And for this reason he could be your most valuable friend, or most formidable foe.

This is not to say that all practitioners of Zen will achieve total "Oneness" with the "Unified Whole" in a given period, but one's understanding of Zen is cumulative from lifetime to lifetime, so you may already be well on your way.... Zen is a way of life. The more it is followed the freer you will become, and it is probably the most avant-garde way of living this side of the Cosmos.

The Zen way of living and teaching by example is honorable if not remarkable. The master's timely correctness of speech or silence does cut to the heart of the matter. They do not allow their minds to be cluttered with beliefs or dogmas, this keeps them open and clear to nature and to the nature of reality.

Thus, by being fresh, free agents of the earth they are abundantly qualified in demonstrating to others, the qualities of naturalness, wholeness, integration and correctness in whatever they are teaching. These qualities lead the Zen beginner to an awareness of God, because God is all of these qualities in manifestation.

This knowledge of God expands in the consciousness of the student as unfolding revelation in truth and enlightenment, and sets him on the path of righteousness.

A Zen master or advanced student is unquestionably more aware of God than the inflexible fundamentalist churchgoer today who still sees himself as separate from his source.

God can always be found in nature, that is why monks and solitaries throughout the ages have sought him there....

Remember this, although the presence of God never departs from nature, he does have to withdraw from some congregations and churches!

Chapter 66

The Immature Soul

THAT an individual could master himself and his world into constructive ends, without first acknowledging and properly channeling his freewill or "allotted energies" to meet those ends, is impossible.

In fact, the history of any given "life-stream" could be better understood if we look at it as the outplaying of the correct and incorrect use of freewill over a time space continuum....

Correctly qualified energy returns to one's "Oversoul" and remains there as one's treasure in heaven. This positive Karma can be likened to a spiritual bank account that can be drawn on in times of need, or to create any positive thing we wish to accomplish. It resides there as the "Sum Total" of our lives and can help and assist us in our present endeavors. It can be seen as "the wind in our sails" that carries us aloft, keeps us above the fray, and moves us forward....

Misqualified energy returns to the "individual" as a debt on the balance sheets and can take many forms. This negative Karma may present in our lives as adversity, challenges to be overcome, difficulties that seem to arise out of nowhere, illness, obligations, setbacks, and even timing issues that may offer or preclude new opportunities..., but these forms are usually the result of greater amounts of misqualified energy that is being returned. The Hindus know this as the "Law of Karma."

Jesus summed up the matter of Karma quite nicely in his statement "what you sow, that shall you also reap." This truth leaves very little room for ambiguity or misinterpretation. Returning Karma is an opportunity to balance the books, so that our energies and works can be rectified and made right. So that we may become more than we are!

For the average man or woman in the street, who has turned the corner, and are doing their best to live correctly, the returning energy will simply manifest as an imperceptible weight upon their shoulders that has been added to their current obligations, and it melds into the current energies we are utilizing so that it can be reused correctly, and thus, sent to the repository of "Good Works" in our "Oversouls."

Returning energies should be seen as a "Gift of God," whereby we are being given a second chance to make things right. The errors of our past are no reason for us to quit the race. Our debts can be repaid, our losses can be recouped. It is the mercy of God, and it is available to all members of the Human Race.

And that's the gist of it. We are all runners in the Human Race, heading towards the finish line, where the Overcomers will be given the gold, a "Crown of Gold" to be exact.

Fret not, dear friends, it is a long race, and you've only been sidelined for awhile! But it is high time to get back into the race, and finish it! The goal is in sight, the finish line is just around the corner. That is what this "Book" is all about!

The individual's use of freewill is now seen as the foremost determining factor in molding one's life. The tool to be used to wield and complete thy perfect creation, and hopefully in creating a pattern of living that will be an example and inspiration to others. One that accords with the Master's plan!

Chapter 67

The Mature Soul

THE event that an individual or society could flourish into its original intent of perfection, without first becoming moral or righteous in the process is completely implausible.

Morality is cleanliness and decency in thought, speech and deed in regard to oneself, in relation to the greater self, God, the progenitor and sustainer of life. Morality is the flower of the soul which blossoms in its own time, and is therefore, the fruit or virtue of a soul's growth and maturity.

In this light, it is clear to see the futility of trying to impose some morals on the immature and young at heart, especially the higher spiritual ones to the spiritually immature. God does not rush the bud to become a flower nor expect adult understanding from a child. Instead, he tends the shoot daily, supporting in any way he can, but allowing the plant to develop into its own inherent beauty.

Of course, pruning is the responsibility of the "Master Gardener" and is sometimes necessary in order to yield more fruit. However, the soul is allowed the time and freedom it needs to develop its own distinctive traits.

This does not mean that we should not set forth good examples to the young and immature, on the contrary, every benign example influences others, but people must be given a certain amount of space and freedom in which to exercise their freewill, so that they may determine what sort of fruit their actions bring....

Morality is much more than a system of beliefs and values created by society and handed down from generation to generation for our consumption. Rather, morality is a collective wisdom of mature souls that have gone before us that has been compiled for our benefit.

As we partake of the fruit of the "Tree of Knowledge," we learn that all actions bring forth effects. We then begin by setting into motion the correct actions, in order to bring about the desired effects.

Thus, with understanding we begin to create a pure and harmonious world around us, produced by the individual yet benefiting the whole, through right living, the offspring of morality!

Chapter 68

The Sacred Sound

MUSIC is spiritual in essence. It is the harmonics of the spheres brought into physical manifestation for the inspiration and upliftment of all. All true music carries the seed of regeneration in its wake. The very foundation of classical music is based on order and discipline in order to achieve integral harmony....

Harmony is the movement of order.

Hence, music is a constructive emanation out of the soundless sound, the "Sacred Om." This is the original intent of music. It is a living reminder of "Etheric Realms" that stirs the heart to longing. It is the sound of the "One," calling us home....

But harmony is not only to be found in classical music. It is not exclusive to any one genre. The principle requirement is that the creators of the music become "Attuned" to the "Life Force," which is a spiritual connection, and not just technique. In rare instances, a progressive band will come along and break all barriers, and infuse harmony into their musical compositions in splendid and complex ways..., and it can be fierce....

"Living music Integrates!"
"Dead music Disintegrates!"
Living music is "In Tune" with the "Life Force!"
Dead music is "Out of Tune" with the "Life Force!"
Living music "Integrates your Life Forces" through "Harmony!"
Dead music "Disintegrates your Life Forces" through "Disharmony!"

Nowadays you can listen to music while you eat, while you bath, while you dress, even while you sleep....

You wake up to music, you listen to music on your way to work, and you have music playing in the background at your office or job, you go to lunch and listen to music while you eat, while you make phone calls, while you wait, you listen to music on your way home, you listen to music whenever your television is on, during the commercials....

It makes you wonder why nearly every business, establishment or place of social gathering pipes in this ungodly stuff whenever and wherever they can, instead of wisely using silence in the background, which is undoubtedly more pleasant, regenerative and productive. It may simply be ignorance on their part. It may be something more....

But the saddest revelation of all is that most of the music you are listening to is not true music at all, it is chatter and noise, and it is a perversion of the "Sacred Sound!"

Thus, you and your families have been subjected to a spiritual kind of death and disintegration through the use of destructive and disharmonious sound that pervades and inundates the whole world....

There is an obvious reason for all this, those who are making the music know not "whence the music cometh." Listen to the Guard's masterpiece called "Promised Land" and you'll find out where the music comes from, and subsequently, the rage! A word of caution though, the concepts of what is truly "Holy" and "Sacred" in this world has been corrupted. This piece of music, in particular, as it was originally released, accomplishes two avant-garde objectives. It performs the "Holy Annunciation," the arrival of "I," the "One," the "Last Prophet!" Secondly, it performs an "expurgation" of the listener. You have been warned!

Why, at the risk of being misunderstood, do I disclose such information? The answer is fourfold. I am addressing the churchgoer and non-churchgoer alike, as well as the youth and posterity, to state the record, to open your minds, and to enrich your lives.

Sound is more delicate and more powerful than most people can imagine. It is more constructive or destructive than they can fathom. Sound can stimulate life at the atomic level, or it can shut it down! This is precisely what destructive sound does to one's finely tuned spiritual body. Sound has the ability to raise life up, or to send it crashing down. Great composers of the past knew this, and they had a respect tantamount to it.

Today, you have a multitude of guitar slinging imposters and drum bangers who have no idea where the "Sacred Sound" comes from, and no respect for themselves, never mind of their music....

The criteria for determining which type of music you are being subjected to is that you "feel its effects." How does it affect your emotions and wellbeing, how does it influence your thoughts and actions, and what does it do to your heart? Do you feel cohesion or a pulling apart? Do you feel an increase or a decrease in your comfort? Do you feel a wholesome structure, or the lack thereof? Do you feel a harmonizing construction or an unsettling destruction?

Incidentally, if one were to omit discipline and order from musical compositions, they would also lack harmony because they would not be attuned to the music of the spheres.

This being such, they would be lacking the qualities of upliftment and regeneration as well, the very qualities your "Life Forces" require for your well-being, the original purpose of the "Sacred Sound" itself.

Any genre of music that does not possess the vital qualities of cohesion and harmony, in essence, would be an aborted music, a dead music because it has severed the thread of "Attunement" with the music of the spheres, the living "Om," which is the "Hum of Life," the "Sacred Sound" of the universe.

The result of such dead music upon an individual is grave indeed, upon a society, drastic. And even for the planetary body that strives to regenerate itself daily in order to sustain life, in turn is repeatedly torn down and raped with destructive rhythm....

In fact, the only quality that aborted music projects is degeneration, resulting in spiritual death to the individual, the society, and to the planetary body at large. In order for a society to live, its music must live. The same goes for the individual, for there can be no regenerative ascending life without spirit!

CHAPTER 69

THE STIR OF ENCHANTMENT

WOULD you know the key to compatibility?
Would you know the essence of good relationships?
Would you hear the secret to finding true joy in life?

Which is your vocation of longing, or your most desired livelihood?
Which qualities stir you to enchantment and love of life?
Which is your most cherished activity..., which is to die for?

Which pursuits do you dream of, what do you truly wish for?
Which trade personifies that essence, which skill embodies that quality?
An artist..., an athlete..., a healer..., a fighter..., a thinker..., a writer...?

The lover of romance loves the romantic!
The surest way to a poet's heart is through a poem!
And to reach the heart of a dancer, one should be a dancer!

Chapter 70

The Unnatural Mind

ALL under heaven and far down along the path,
After many a trial won, and the illusions of the world overcome,
We still clear ourselves of webs....

A condition of standing still...,
And I have yet to see a spider spin a web upon a rolling wheel!
Hence, the secret of ridding oneself of pests....

We must be moving even in our stillness,
And steady as we move....
Standstill and movement are activities of mind!

As everything in nature ebbs and flows continuously,
Of what consequence is a mind that stops?
Or lodges itself between two poles of thought?

A mind that stops is no longer free!
Movement and freedom are one!
And a mind that is not free imprisons the individual!

Chapter 71

The Wheel of Mind

AND as if that were not enough...,
One dark and desolate night when you are alone...,
The hemispheres of your mind will unhinge...,
You will stand upon that thin line of rationale,
Your sanity and stability tested,
Your fears come upon you....

And what would the result to an individual be,
If he were to settle down upon his fears,
Imprisoned by a mind that cannot move...,
A mind that has become stuck...?
The wheel of the mind...,
Must be able to roll past its fears and out of the mire!

Chapter 72

The Natural Mind

PARADOX...,

"One cannot attain liberation *without* controlling the mind...,
But one cannot control the mind *without* letting it go!"

Paradox...,

"The mind cannot be controlled *by* retaining it!"

Paradox...,

"The factor of control and balance...,
Is built into the very framework of Cosmos...,
Yet *nothing* is static....
Nothing is retained and *everything* is controlled!"

Summary...,

When everything *is* allowed to flow naturally, everything *is* free,
Because *Freedom* and *Movement* are *one* and the same!

Hence, the enlightened man holds back no quarter of himself,
And becomes *one* with the Unified Whole!

CHAPTER 73

THE TURNABOUT

TO be possessive of something, be it life, wealth, family or fame requires by law that we should lose it, because it is not being held on to correctly, that is, by an enlightened and selfless love, but rather in a selfish manner....

Haven't you seen those blessed individuals who have not much to hold on to, but out of sheer kindness would give away that which they have? Yet, contrarily, these are the ones who never seem to run out of things, there is a universal supply of stuff at their disposal..., meanwhile, the unwise scheme, strive and cling to hold on to their stuff....

Jesus spoke of a woman who gave away all she had. These are examples of the "Law of Detachment" at work. The "Law of Detachment" is also a major paradox in that it dictates, if you would hold on to something, you should let it go. If you would possess something, you should give it away.

In this way, nothing is kept static, nothing is retained and everything is allowed to flow naturally to its proper place.

This is why they say "the only things you can take with you when you leave this earth are the things you have given away." Detachment is now seen as a tool that can affect every aspect of your lives, the more important the object, the greater the detachment. The more I want to experience God, the more I have to let him go....

One does not possess life or God by clinging to them. The fruit that becomes ripe lets go of the vine, the soul that becomes wise lets go of life, and obtains life everlasting!

Chapter 74

The Separation

THERE is no place for selfishness,
In a Cosmos where everything,
Belongs to God....

Of what consequence,
Are your petty possessions?
And obsessions!

Surrender unto God what is rightfully his...,
He will surrender unto you what is rightfully yours...,
And you will have mended the separation....

After all,
That which is rightfully yours, can never be lost...,
That which is not, can never be kept....

Loose your hold...,
Allow things to flow...,
Back to you!

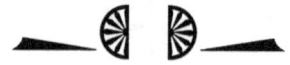

Chapter 75

The Separate Self

SELFISHNESS and oneness are but opposing states of consciousness and awareness, albeit arising from the same principle. The "Rule of Oneness" is the natural state and "Code" of the Cosmos, thus, there is no other. Whether you refer to this "Rule" as the principle of unity, togetherness or wholeness, the "Rule" remains intact, the affliction of selfishness is one of understanding on behalf of the individual that results in the separation....

Selfishness is the unnatural by product of an individual's state of mind that arises when one senses oneself to be a separate entity in a world of objects. Therefore, the affliction of mind arises out of the individual's sense of separateness from the natural "Rule of Oneness!"

To relinquish selfishness is not to lose the self, but rather to gain a Cosmos! It is to become integrated into the universal grid in a most harmonious way....

The eternal grid of which we are linked is a finely intermeshed weave. The whole of creation is like a tapestry that is the Creator's handiwork. Everything that exists in the "Creation" whether animated or inanimate could be called a strand within that weave. We likewise, are strands within that intricate weave, so if one were to sense oneself as separate from the Creator's handiwork, it would not only be an affliction, it would be a cardinal sin as well. A cardinal sin is a sin that denies its most fundamental part, in regard to man, a sin in which the created denies its Creator. It is an offense to God that his creation would separate their selves from him, regardless that it arises from their states of mind....

Therefore, to see and sense oneself as separate from the Creator, in a Cosmos where everything is a "Unified Whole," is to be wholly under the influence of Maya, the Hindu word for illusion, whereby one is drifting in the illusory world of the senses, while forgetting one's source at the same time....

The prescription for the illusion *is* to "Wake Up!"
The prescription for the affliction *is* to seek "Oneness!"

Oneness is the natural by product of an individual who knows his self to be one with all that is, immersed in the "Matrix of Creation." Oneness is the state of realization of the "Awakened" individual who begins to see through the world of appearances.... Upon awakening from the dream of Maya, one begins to sense oneself as the center and ground of the universe.

When the slumbering youth begins to break the shell of illusion, that is, of separation, selfishness is soon forsaken..., "Oneness" dawns in the mind of the neophyte, for the Cosmos has ever been but "One!"

Chapter 76

The Microcosmic Self

ACHIEVING the state of "Oneness" is the necessary precondition to achieving the state of "Selflessness." You must first sense yourself within the whole, before you can let go of the self. Letting go of the microcosmic self or "Individual Self" is tantamount to the raindrop slipping into the shining sea.... It is to lose oneself in the undulating currents in the ocean of God, the fascinating thing is, that one actually finds oneself instead. Individuality is not lost, it is gained, and one becomes a permanent "Focus" of awareness in the macrocosmic self or "Body of God."

Soon the sensation of selflessness buoys one up to the realization that, "nothing more needs to be done that is not already being done, and that all living is a playful and joyous air."

Becoming "Selfless" means that you will no longer be buffeted about by the elements, but will begin rolling with them....

Selfhood must first be attained before you can dismiss the self, and true selfhood is realized in the state of "Oneness." Unless true "Oneness" is attained, all seeming selflessness is mere lack of identity and of mediocre proportion. For one is not yet conscious or capable of containing his portion, never mind letting it go!

 The Macrocosmic Self

TO relinquish the microcosmic self is to gain the macrocosmic self. It is to surrender a part in order to gain a whole.

But, it is another thing altogether to realize that the self you are surrendering has never been apart from the whole, and that your part is actually his part, it is to offer to God that which is already his.... Thus, it restores the divine equation!

To relinquish the self means to relinquish all desires that have hold on the self. The acquiring of wealth, the accumulation of power, and the unbridled ambition is simply solidified desire in the process of becoming habit....

To retain any measure of desire means that you are retaining a portion of the self in which to house that desire, unless it is good, righteous and congruent with Gods. In retaining that portion of the self, regardless of how well hidden it may be, is to sacrifice selflessness. It is to remain a separate "Individual Self" within the "Unified Whole" still operating under the illusion of Maya....

The microcosmic self that desires remains separate from the macrocosmic self, while the self that lets go of desire attains "Oneness."

To experience true "Oneness" with the Creator, is to see the folly of selfish desire, is to slip into the sea of selflessness!

Chapter 78

The Master's Vessel

Shakespeare wrote,

"When the sea was calm,
All ships alike,
Showed mastership in floating...."

The ship is the soul!
Freewill the navigator!
Truth is the compass!
God is the goal!

The four elements are now harnessed...,
All sails are in the wind...,
Onward, my dear soul...,
Your Creator draweth nigh....

Chapter 79

The Master

NO desire rolls me,
When Maya tries to control me,
As much as she can!

At last, the upheavals and fleeting chases,
Storms and bows breaking,
Have mainly subsided....

I am becoming the master of my ship,
But, pray tell me,
In what condition is my ship?

CHAPTER 80

THE ASSESSMENT

I NEED peace and quiet,
And time to assess,
Myself....

The pounding waves and gales of life,
Have battered and washed away,
All that was not tied down....

It shall take some time to ascertain,
To what extent my damaged body,
Mind and soul has undergone....

What good qualities remain...?
What true values retained...?
What flaws removed...?

Chapter 81

The Mortal Grid

WHITHER will the wind blow tomorrow?
Where will I find myself upon its rest?
Shall I trace familiar steps into my dreary past?
To sit forlorn, dejected, devoid of zest?

Or shall the winds decide to whisk me away,
To new heights so that I might drift,
Into new circumstances, make new,
All I know to be true, the errors sifted?

May of necessity there be no wind,
To usher me up again, could this state,
Be my final resting place, a mortal remain,
Subject to death, but who to blame?

If after long last my abode is dust?
Let me clarify one thing at least...,
Chance and accidents are lies, creation is just,
We lie in the beds that we have made!

Chapter 82

The Immortal Grid

LUCRETIUS said, "Nothing comes from nothing!" This being a significant observation, I ask the following, "How could a state of being, arise out of a state of non-being, or, how could life proceed out of nothingness?"

Life can *only* proceed from life!
Consciousness can *only* proceed from consciousness!

To acknowledge this is to realize that the source of all life, God, could not have come forth from the great void, out of nothingness. But has instead ever been! Life is a constant and a constant changing, as we have not come forth from nothingness, but from the source of eternal life, we are the eternal evolving offspring of "Life" itself, which is no less than the "Creator" itself. We are chips off the old block....

The event that we call death does not entail a cessation of life. It entails a change of situation, a change of face, place, plane and expression. We are living in a segment of eternity now and eternity wears many masks....

The difference between us and the perfected ones is manifold, but basically one of "Psychological Freedom" from the illusion of Maya originating from the lower densities, and a "Spiritual Mastery" resulting from a "Balanced Karma." The ascended ones have achieved "Full Consciousness" with the Creator and have shifted up to that appropriate plane of expression. The immortal ones are no longer bound to the lower planes where desire and duality rule, thus, they have no inordinate desire and are forever free to roam the higher realms of the immortal grid....

We however, must continue to re-embody until perfection is forged, with periods of physical withdrawal, that is, death, in between. The perfected ones have gained eternal freedom, and within the boundless sphere immortally reign!

Chapter 83

The Puzzle

A GOOD teacher,
Weaves words and metaphors...,
Portraits and pictures...,
In order to allow,
Momentary glimpses,
Of a wider reality,

To unfold in the minds,
Of the students,
Thereby adding,
Another piece of the puzzle...,
To human understanding,
Of our cosmic enigma!

Chapter 84

The Message

THIS above all...,
Is your reason for being!
Not merely to write a book,
Make a name, achieve fame,
But to out-picture the Christ!

Carry the flame, be the light...,
And exemplify the scriptures,
Shoulder the cross, bear the burden,
And embody the truth,
Distributing to the need of Saints!

Withstand the yoke...,
And instruct the brethren,
Till death do us part!
And suspend the fruit,
Of Christic attribute!

Chapter 85

The Messenger

OUT of the flame,
And into the world,
Of our domain,
To bring the Word,

To the ill informed,
The hostile aimed,
Perchance to help,
The spiritually lame,

To attain a measure,
Comprehend...,
The wider picture,
To their own ends,

Complete the puzzle,
Tie up loose ends,
Balance the books,
Ere ascend,

By mine example,
In our domain,
Out of the world,
And into the flame!

Chapter 86

 The Rigid

THE problem with most fundamentalists is that they quote scripture to use against people. I contend that perfect thoughts and deeds will eventually get you to heaven. Our works will be tried, there is the import. We must redeem ourselves in God's eyes....

They defend saying...,

> "For by grace are ye saved by faith;
> And that not of yourselves:
> It is the gift of God; not of works,
> Lest any man should boast."

- Ephesians 2: 8, 9

I agree, and reply...,

> "But wilt thou know, O vain man,
> That faith without works is dead?"

- James 2: 20

I would say, externalize your outlook..., edify your brothers and sisters, use and commend scripture to unify each other!

Chapter 87

The Fearful

WHAT is Fear?
What is freedom?

    Fear is insecurity in an insecure world!
    Freedom is the absence of insecurity and of fear itself!

Since all fear is rooted in either consciousness or sub-consciousness, one may be inclined to ask, where did it come from, how did it get there? Who planted the seeds of fear and insecurity in the first place?

Your first Mother and Father did!

    Fear is the product of the "Original Sin" of disobedience!
    Fear is the consequence of the "First Sin" ever committed!
    Insecurity is the by product and "Effect" of fear itself!

Everyone's fall from grace is the result of Adam and Eve's committing of the "Original Sin!" Everyone's fear is the product of the committing of the "First Sin" of disobedience! Everyone's insecurity is the resultant effect of these actions....

Thus the first instance of "Cause and Effect" springs into existence as the result of "Man's Freewill!" Sin is the "Cause," and fear is the "Effect."

    Sin = Cause
    Effect = Fear

What was Adam's first response to the Lord, after partaking of the forbidden fruit, when the Lord came looking for him in the cool of the day...?

> "And the Lord God called unto Adam,
> And said unto him, Where *art* thou?"

- Genesis 3: 9

> "And he said, I heard thy voice in the garden,
> And I was afraid, because I *was* naked; and I hid myself."
>
> - Genesis 3: 10

He was afraid!

The unholy act of committing the "First Sin" of disobedience to God immediately manifested as "Fear" in Adam and Eve. The act of disobeying the "First Commandment" of the "Living God" was tantamount to separating themselves from Him. When Adam and Eve's eyes were opened, they at once sensed themselves as being separate and apart from their Creator, and fear set in. The Devil's ploy had worked. He had managed to separate the created from the Creator. Thus, the Creator cursed the serpent, and man has known the fruit of "Good and Evil" ever since....

Your "Original Sin" was inherited when that old serpent, that silvery tongued Devil tempted your first Mother of the fruit she should have abstained from, when he whispered in her ear and said..., "Ye shall not surely die...," were she to partake of the forbidden fruit....

At that very moment, she distinguished herself from the self of God, as did Adam when he ate of the fruit. And from that point on humanity as a whole has been sensing itself as separate from God, and his Creation.

Adam and Eve, and subsequently the entire "Human Race" have fallen for the "First Lie," the lie that tells us we are separate from our Creator, when in fact we are not separate. Humanity instead is living in fear as the result of the "Original Sin," of disobedience to God that we all have inherited from our first parents, Adam and Eve, and the "Human Race" have been under Satan's spell or lie ever since.

This is our inherited original sin which is also a cardinal sin. We each one need to reverse that original sin, and get out from under Satan's spell. We each one, need to remove that barrier of sin, (not separation) between ourselves and God. We each one, need to make reparations and heal the rift. With contrite hearts and repentant spirits, the illusion of separation will lift, as the barrier of sin is absolved, we will become one with our Creator and his Creation once again....

In regard to fear..., fears are internal things, not external things.... As all seeds produce after their kind, the weeds of fear sprout also, and will overrun your garden and estate if you let them, hence, the need to purge your hearts and minds where thought originates.

Fears are also products of unnatural minds and imperfect thinking that over time produces bad habits, poor judgment and imbalances. Fear results in conditions such as personal complexes, feelings of inferiority or superiority, senses of self-condemnation or self-infatuation..., illogic, irrationality and superstition..., ad infinitum!

Any repetitive way of thinking or acting unwittingly conditions us at the same time. Fear is a conditioned response to insecurity and uncertainty which prevents us from being free, and is therefore of the mind....

As everything that lives grows, and as thoughts are seeds, "your fears will come upon you," because they are rooted in the hidden most recesses of your mind and are being sustained by your lasting insecurities, imbalances, irrationalities and sins.

You must first discover the source of the insecurity or fear, look closely at each one until you recognize the "Cause." Once you recognize the cause it will vanish of its own accord because it is in reality, baseless. It is not tangible, it is not logical, so it cannot persist....

If you determine that your fears stem from yet other "Sins," one would be well advised to "Confess and Renounce" those sins to the Creator with a sincere heart. As the sins are absolved the fears will fade....

Fears are those most enduring things until you look at them closely, then they fade away like a vapor, you realize they were never even there!

In this way, you can uproot the weeds and discard them completely. They will nevermore infest your garden, you will have become free!

Chapter 88

The Day of Judgment

THE work of destruction and creation is one process. By observing nature we can prove this beyond questioning....

The formation of land masses are produced by very destructive volcanoes. The rising and falling of continents are the result of the movement of the underlying plates. The adjusting of the tectonic plates on the ocean floor can cause deadly tsunamis to the inhabitants in its path. The sudden shifting of the poles could roll up heaven and earth as a scroll. The melting of the ice caps affects the salt level in the oceans, making havoc with our climate as a consequence. A forest fire can rape the earth of her beauty. The impact of asteroids can pummel the earth and kill many, while a comet could bring about "Doomsday," and devastate all life on earth, or move the earth out of her place....

Yet, as volcanoes spew lava over miles of land, destroying everything in its wake, it is at the same time, laying a new foundation. A major shifting of the plates could result in the sinking of one continent while raising another. The shifting of the poles is earth's way of maintaining equilibrium in an ever changing environment, it has happened before, it shall happen one more time prior to the new creation. The colder climates will become warm, warmer climates will become cold. The melting of the polar caps will cause earth's oceans to rise, burying many coastal areas, creating new coastal areas. The devastation of a forest fire will reveal an abundance of seedlings and wildflowers the very next spring. Meteors and asteroids could disrupt life on earth, but may also bring seeds of life from other worlds....

Creation, destruction and recreation is a never-ending process that proceeds in cycles.

As man is integral to nature, he is also subject to that process, the cycles of men bear definite periods of destruction at intervals in order to create a new man, a better man.... And even upon the final dissolution of the physical body, and perfection not achieved, the work of improvement goes on. The hand of the clock continues to turn. The earth revolves around the sun. Babies are born. The work of perfection goes on....

Destruction is not the opposite of creation! Destruction is merely the first stages of creation! The "Day of Judgment" must come before the "Day of the New Creation," therefore the "Day of Destruction" must come, before the "Day of the New Creation."

The implosion of our national economy will reverberate around the world and result in a "One World Currency" and economy, only to be followed by a "Moneyless" global economy and society....

Somewhere along the line, an epiphany will take place, followed by a "Global Enlightenment," people will awake to the fact that they no longer want to be slaves to the dollar, pound, deutsche mark or yen.... They will decide to break free from the systems of currency and servitude....

It will dawn on people that "Life" is a "Divine Gift," that is precious, and that they should not have to "Earn" the right to live, or exist in abject poverty.

A system of "Credits" will be devised; the Internal Revenue Service will re-fashion itself as the External Distribution Service whose mandate will be to provide and distribute citizen's "Credits" necessary for them to live, support and thrive within the commonweal.

There will be tiers arranged to determine how the "Credits" will be distributed....

At the first tier, the "Essential" allotment of "Credits" will be sufficient for one to secure lodging, food, clothing, transportation and goods at an essential level....

At the second tier, for those who enjoy the "Fruits of the Labor," those who choose to be the invaluable cogs in the wheels that keep the machinery and systems running by providing vital services to the commonweal, will be given a "Vital" allotment of "Credits" that will allow them to secure lodging, food, clothing, transportation and goods at a luxury level....

The top tier will be reserved for the Artists and Academia, the Writers, Poets and Thinkers, the Professors, Scholars and Scientists, the Musicians and Performers, the Creators, Designers and Engineers.... These will be given the "Creative" allotment of "Credits" that will allow them to secure lodging, food, clothing, transportation and goods of the most "Exclusive and Select" kinds. They will have the freedom to live and move about as they choose at a Carte-Blanche level, as they provide the Art, Beauty, Knowledge, Music, Dance, Inspiration and Design that all members of the commonweal cherish and enjoy, that indeed make "Life Worth Living...."

This "Credit System" will begin in the United States and become the model for a "Global Moneyless System," that will end poverty and disadvantage and transform "Planet Earth" into a "Galactic Wonder," and it will provide the "Free Citizen" with the means and initiative to prosper....

Those in the "Essential" sector who receive the "Essential" allotment of "Credits" can decide to enjoy the "Fruits of the Labor" by joining the "Vital" sector.... Thus they will begin providing necessary services to the commonweal and to their fellowman.... They will move up to a luxury level of living enjoyed by those in the "Vital" sector.... For those who are artistically or creatively inclined, they will gravitate to the "Creative" level, thus, achieving and enjoying the "Best Life Has to Offer!"

The ancient Mayans were the timekeepers of "Father Time." They devised a calendar that predicted the exact day the world would end, December 21, 2012.... At which time the sun would pass through the dark rift of the Milky Way in the galactic center of the heavens.

The recently discovered *"Lost Book of Nostradamus"* describes the alignment of the constellations in the heavens during this period with the imagery of an eight-spoked wheel. An alignment that cannot be determined without introducing Ophiuchus, the thirteenth hidden sign of the zodiac.... Using this alignment, Nostradamus predicts a "twenty-year period" wherein the world will encounter great upheavals and face great challenges that could bring an end to the world as we know it, December 21, 1992 to December 21, 2012. He also names an enigmatic persona known only as "One Male."

The Hopi Indian tribe of native North America warns of dire consequences arising from the "Day of the Great Purification" of "Mother Earth" at the end of time....

But by far, mankind's truest and most solemn prophecies concerning the "End of Time" come from John the Revelator, who wrote the divinely inspired book of Revelation, the last book in the *"Holy Bible."*

This book unseals and expounds upon the scriptures contained in the book of Revelation.

One thing is for sure, the "Day of Tribulation" cometh! Not only are we living in the twenty-year period that Nostradamus talks about, we are in the last quarter of that timeframe. Whether the events leading up to the inevitable day of "God's Wrath" occurs tomorrow, or anytime prior to December 21, 2012, the prognosis is the same, now is the appointed time for salvation!

But the "Day of Judgment" was designed for the souls of men. The true import of the "Day of Judgment" has been ordained on high from the beginning, because the end was known from the beginning, in that it dictates that the acts of men, both individually and collectively shall be called to account. "The Lord's Day" was conceived so that God's children could be gathered up at the time of the end, which is the harvest of souls....

All that is coming about on the earth, all that shall happen on a global scale and all that has been ordained in the lives of men, are the consequences of the "Day of Judgment!"

Chapter 89

The Day of Desolation

PAIN....
Poverty...,
And natural catastrophe,
Are the great equalizers of men!

Whereby,
One is brought into solemn confrontation...,
With the stark human condition!
The world is a very severe teacher to the ungodly!

Disaster....
Doomsday...,
And annihilation,
Are the rewards of Godlessness!

Chapter 90

# The Evildoer and the Liar

DECEIT..., deceit..., deceit....

"When the abomination of desolation stands in the holy place..."

Companies are *cheating* workers...,
Workers are *cheating* companies...,
Companies are *cheating* companies!

Friends are *lying* to friends...,
Neighbors are *lying* to neighbors...,
Strangers are *lying* to strangers!

Leaders are *deceiving* leaders...,
Governments are *deceiving* governments...,
Nations are *deceiving* nations!

Siblings are *corrupting* siblings...,
Parents are *corrupting* families...,
Families are *corrupting* God's "*Holy Church!*"

Men are *violating* women...,
Women are *violating* themselves...,
Mates are *violating* God's "*Holy Matrimony!*"

Priests are *desecrating* children...,
Teachers are *desecrating* students...,
Surgeons are *desecrating* God's "*Holy Temples!*"

Man is *abusing* man...,
Man is *abusing* humanity...,
Man is *abusing* God's "*Holy Creation!*"

Chapter 91

The Blessing and the Curse

THE closer we draw to God,
The more blessed we become,
Though not infrequent it be,
A blessing from God,
May awaken a curse from man...,
Still the sun shines....

I have been told that the gift of discernment,
Is a blessing of the fortunate one!
So I kneel and pray for mine enemies,
And for their deliverance,
For only God knows...,
I cannot help but discern....

CHAPTER 92

THE TRUE ISRAELITE

HOW can you tell a "True Israelite" from a false one? The prerequisite is that you first acknowledge that there are false ones.... From the very beginning, there have been imposters masquerading as the true Israelites. It is not a name, or a cause, or a race that determines who or what a "True Israelite" is..., so I will tell you....

A "True Israelite" is a "True Believer" in the divinity of "Man," and in the "Holy Trinity," that is, "God the Father," "God the Son," and "God the Holy Spirit." That "God the Father" dwelt bodily in his "Son" Jesus Christ, and that his "Son" was sent to earth for the redemption of Mankind! Any disbelief of the aforementioned would preclude one from being a "True Believer" and incidentally, from being a "True Israelite!"

Additionally, a "True Israelite" refuses to take someone else's portion! He would avoid needless chatter and handshakes, and pats on the back. He would abhor talking for the sake of talking, and does not participate in illusive topics, he is however, expected to listen to them. He speaks mainly on matters of truth, and his words and intent are without guile, he knows how and when to cut to the root of one's misconceptions in order to enlighten them, though it often goes unheeded, his timing is swift, he is a master of excision. The "True Israelite" conserves himself and is discreet in his conservation. He has manners, and appreciates the manners of others. He has a keen sense of all that is "Holy," and bestows the proper respect. He likewise, has sensors that allow him to detect anything unclean, and avoids those things at all costs.

The "True Israelite" is a "Light-Bearer" who brings wisdom and illumination to the world. They are the "Salt of the Earth!" They are the "Keeper of the Keys!" They are the "Expounders of the Wisdom!" It is not because of these things that they are the "Chosen People," they are these things because they are the "Chosen People!"

The "True Israelite" today is scattered over the face of the whole earth, as a result of the process known as the "Transmigration of Souls." They are not confined to any specific race or nation! A "True Israelite" must always sit under his own vine and fig tree! Nothing else will suffice!

Chapter 93

The Discriminator

WHY is it that we shy away from some individuals, while we are drawn to others? Why is it that we feel a certain uncomfortable-ness in the presence of some people, while we feel a sense of safety and security in the presence of others? Why is it that a few rare acquaintances can make your knees tremble, or make you cringe upon a chance encounter?

The unfailing sense and faculty of discrimination that determines who is safe and who is not for the clean hearted aspirant on the path, is the ability to "Feel" the "Auric Emanations" of others. It is the "Gut" that lets us know what kind of person we are meeting, and what kind of energies they are utilizing; it likewise lets us know what sort of place or situation we are entering into....

It is no mistake that the "Gut" and the "Soul" occupy the same place in the "Human Frame!" This is where expressions such as "Gut Instinct" or "Gut Reaction" come from.... You may even refer to it as "Soul Wisdom!"

Words may deceive but the stomach does not lie! The soul is the center of discernment for the spiritual type, and its warnings should not be ignored. It is the actual sounding board of psychic energies!

CHAPTER 94

THE DIVISION

I SIT under an azure sky. It's sapphire canopy un-obscured by clouds. Intuition is similarly clear and potent today. A bit of psychology emerges as the Christ mind and the mind of the world interact....

The Christ mind respects other sentient beings by knowing that we are "One" in essence. That we all originate from the same source. The worldly mind respects the Christ principle on an inner level, but does not understand it consciously on an outer level. As all individuals differ in understanding, and in levels of attainment and attunement, some people sense this inner recognition immediately, others, a couple of hours or a day, but seldom more than a day.

At once, they are attracted to the Christ presence, but soon become sort of uncomfortable, and so they kindly resist. The worldly watch and observe those of the Christ mind curiously, yet, they all come to similar answers raised by asking themselves similar questions. Such as, who is this person? What is it that is different about him? Then they reassure themselves saying, he is just another person, a low-key quiet type perhaps, but through his manner, speech and kindness, and subsequent lack of worldliness, coarseness and vulgarity, they inevitably return and ask themselves, who is this person?

So they continue to observe and study and interact. Soon, the soul (solar) friction raises more questions, like, is he dangerous? Does he present a threat? Yes, the thought of danger does cross their minds, for whenever a human being cannot easily plumb the depths of another, or understand the foundation of which he functions, a moment of danger ensues....

But at this point, there arises equilibrium. Their souls convince them that these individuals are not at all dangerous. In fact, they are rather harmless, meek even....

Thus, the wise tutor of the soul slowly and positively informs them consciously, so as to put forth this conclusion.... I know what I see..., I know what I hear..., but mostly..., I know what I feel.... I feel, therefore I know, that this person is just the opposite of a dangerous person, and then they suddenly realize or awake to the fact that this person is very, very good!

This is what Christ meant when he said, "I come not to bring peace, but a sword." This "Sword" is real, and this "Division" is real, it is palpable to the very bones and is no more avoidable than night or day, it simply is....

The living example of Christ is the "Sword" that sunders unreality from reality, the world of the senses from the world of the soul.

With all of this then, does not Christ present a real threat and a danger indeed to those who are yet comfortable in the world!

CHAPTER 95

THE SWORD OF TRUTH

THE day of intimidation is spent,
The basic concerns of vestment, food and rent,
All needs of the mortal coil bent...,
Straight lies my path!

Enough pleasing a worldly boss,
To hear oral gifts of dead praise,
They thinking it a reasonable toss...,
Proceed to steal my strength!

The time of compromise is past,
I shall speak the truth and act,
Sword of truth unsheathed at last...,
Beware purveyors of untruth!

Like sword of Damocles suspended,
Poised bright and steely white,
In the summer, an unexpected rain...,
Flash of lightning strike!

Chapter 96

The Hardened

WHERE has all compassion gone?
Why just this morning,
I picked up a newspaper,
Challenger victims honored...,
Five hundred missing in Bangladesh....

The six o'clock news tells us,
Poor babies are dying from aids,
But we are closer to curing cancer,
Five thousand Afghans slain...,
Miss Jane has won another Oscar....

Old news, well change the channel,
Tommy is being operated on today,
If only we could locate his family,
But Lisa gets along well, no one can tell...,
She's got one leg....

A bit dull, turn the knob,
Anti-abortionists planting bombs,
Guerrillas seize Lebanon,
Suzy didn't come home today...,
Padres lose it in the ninth....

I will tell you where all compassion has gone,
The onslaught of the world has killed it....
But hear me friends...,
People are starving in the streets, dying for a bite to eat...,
Just beyond the swap meet!

CHAPTER 97

THE NEEDFUL

LOVE is not something beyond our control...,
Love does not depend upon likes and dislikes,
Even less does it depend upon beauty!
Love depends upon mutual need...,
A need recognized by two parties,
Who join in agreement to supply each others need....

Today, I saw two homeless ones...,
The down and out, the outcasts,
Shoeless and weather worn, unkempt...,
But the woman held on to the hand...,
Of the man who kissed her cheek,
Sitting on a sidewalk oblivious to the goings-on around them....

There was no beauty apparent...,
No vanity to be attached to,
Nothing one could give to the other...,
That they didn't already possess...,
Nothing left but the basic need, to banish loneliness....
In the end, we love the one that is available!

CHAPTER 98

THE ABUSERS

THE New Year faithfully rings in a new day!
Bird song delightfully fills the air,
Around I see trees dancing and gay,
Flowers of hope would passersby share,
Oh why does man delay?

Elementals join in.... God's left them gifted,
The planet is lighter today...,
As beings stand tall, the baggage lifted,
The pure in heart sing roundelay,
The Snows of January has darkness evicted!

Mother knows Father will mitigate,
The karmic load on earth...,
Though Mother herself never Father disgraced,
She has carried the burden of men since birth,
Who yet misuse the Father's grace!

Four elements of God in balanced fusion,
Fire and air and water and earth,
The awesome power of nature uses,
For in all the myriad forms of nature,
Only man or woman abuses!

Chapter 99

The Stream

I WOULD disabuse your minds,
And liberate your worlds,
By setting straight...,
The facts from the fiction!

Life is eternal, and you are life!
Consciousness is a continuous stream!
The physical world appears and disappears!
The incorporeal mind ever remains!

By the means of freewill,
Man can choose to live,
Or choose to die...,
No one else may decide!

Man can muddy the stream of mind,
Until it becomes sewer material,
When the mind is a sewer...,
Man's home is the sewer!

Man can purify the stream of mind,
Until it is congruent with God's mind....
When man's mind becomes Godlike...,
Man is at home with God!

Man creates or miscreates his world,
After the desires of his heart!
Therein, will you find the manifold sorrows of mankind!
And the path of liberation!

Chapter 100

The Unjust Stewards

WHY is it that some people exude life, while others exude death? Why is it that everything seems to fall together for some people, while everything seems to fall apart for others? Why is it that some individuals have much beneficial fruit to extend to others, while some individuals seem pale, barren and devoid of any life sustaining fruit?

Regardless of the fact, that the races of men have been bred and crossbred, combined, intertwined and manipulated for thousands of years..., there is such a thing as soul accountability. Man is responsible for his creation and his works! God is not mocked, nor is his creation subject to "Causes and Effects" outside of the "Law!"

My worldly mind defends saying, sure, humankind is as diverse as the wildflowers on the plains, but did even one choose its own traits or qualities? A multitude of men and women have gone through all manner of hardship, obstacles and adversity, and although you may not feel quite right around some of them, is it, after all, a man's fault for what he is? Yes, there are those who have entered into the gateway of life by less than ideal means, many horrific, and many untold numbers have been conceived through adultery, deceit, and violence.... Could there not be, at least a few, who are victims of bad blood, inferior seed, or misfortunate breeding? How, after all, can you judge them for who they are, or what they have become?

True, many have entered into life despite the odds and have passed through great adversity, but the "Wheel of the Law," and the "Wisdom of the Son" infallibly settles the debate saying, "Be Not Deceived," what thou hast sown yesterday is today reaping. The "Wheel of Justice" has never lagged and continues to turn perfectly, and so sustains the "Law of Karma."

Each one is "Solely Responsible" and "Held Accountable" for the "State of their Souls," which is also their "Estate," be it an estate of "Paradise" or of "Plight." The "Young Soul" with "Little Knowledge" shall be treated accordingly..., even as the "Old Soul" with "Great Knowledge." Nay, none are excusable! The issue is "How" they have used it....

In the beginning, God's light shone upon all creation equally, today it shines upon the just and the unjust!

Chapter 101

 The Temple

AND so all responsibility shifts back to the builder,
The whole task of this earthly life,
Is to lay the foundation of "Righteousness,"
Erect the structure of "God's Will,"
And build the temple of "Holiness,"
The "Right Use" of "God's Will" leads to "Holiness!"

Have you ever seen an unfinished home?
Unstable foundations...,
Solid foundations with faulty structure...,
Sound structure bereft of walls...,
Even the very best plans are useless unless completed...,
Neither give shelter, none protects, they are uninhabitable!

The skills of the Architect transcend the physical,
They are the rudimentary skills of life...,
Without a temple to house the soul,
You are yet a homeless soul....
God provides the real estate, but you must build the estate...,
Be therefore an Architect of light!

Everything is simple if you start from the beginning,
First, you must draw up the plans...,
Second, you must gather up all your resources...,
Third, you must build the temple!
Once completed, you can "Light a Fire" that will not be extinguished....
A truly "Energy Efficient" home secure from the elements!

Chapter 102

The Soul

EVERY act you have ever committed,
Every word uttered forth, spoken or unspoken...,
Every thought framed in mind, every impression,
All joy, suffering, hope, despair....

All hell you have ever experienced,
All heaven sacrificed...,
Every mistake made,
Was no mistake at all!

Rather, only the means to bring you,
To one unmistakable end...,
To awake to the realization,
That the right use of God's will,

Is the right way to live!
Truthfully, not one incident extra,
Not one second less...,
The whole cornucopia of experience,

Was ordained and designed,
To set your feet upon the path today!
Like a rose, it is an individual process...,
That blossoms in its own time!

Only when you consciously set your feet upon the path,
Does the goal of your soul emerge!
At last, the great work of the ages...,
The "Grand Design" reveals!

Chapter 103

The Dyad

OPEN, receptive, letting it go...,
She is the Holy Chalice....
Spacious, yielding, accepting, reeling...,
The sea lies within the "Woman!"

Full, contained, letting it flow...,
He is the Sacred Vessel....
Firm, devising, providing, rushing...,
The river lies within the "Man!"

In the image of God created he him...,
Male and Female created he them....
Solid, unified, balanced, whole...,
The future belongs to the "Dyadic Twin!"

Chapter 104

The Shepherd

THERE are no more philosophers,
And consequently no philosophies!
What's more, they are no longer necessary, thank God....

The long, dark trek through the centuries,
Of pain and toil of interpretation,
Has not been in vain....

We have arrived at the age of truth,
Aquarius! And it carries a violet hue....
That truth expands with the advent of Aquarius,

And presses upon the heart,
Of the just made perfect by love...,
Thus, it awaits you....

The second coming of Christ occurs,
As the expansion of "Trinities' Flame,"
Upon the temple's altar when the soul is ripe....

Inasmuch as all figs...,
Do not mature and fall at once...,
It is an individual process!

CHAPTER 105

THE HERD

EVERYWHERE I go,
Astounded by triviality,
The herds rant and rave...,
In search of idle play!

Everyone is comfortable,
Chattering away about,
Worthless things...,
All the day....

And into the night,
They tumble and gyrate,
Intoxicate...,
Till morning light!

All their lives,
Spent in haste,
A meaningless waste...,
Killing time....

How long oh Lord,
Canst thou endure,
This blinded age...,
That ignores you?

Chapter 106

The Hollow

IN and around,
This alien town...,
Nothing of worth,
Lost or found...,
Here abounds!

Some would say,
In a smug way,
That nothing of worth,
Ever stood ground...,
Above or below the hollow town!

Others would jest,
And gleefully test...,
The optimists,
By generally stating,
Nothing of worth!

Few would attest,
With illumined zest...,
That nothing of worth,
Ever stemmed from lips...,
Of vacant pessimists!

CHAPTER 107

THE THREAD

THIS battle of principalities is exhaustive,
So I must place the planes in proper perspective...,
Yes, you may have the authority of the workplace,
So I render you your mortal authority...,
Render me your mortal respect!

However, all true authority stems from the immortal,
That hierarchical chain of which I am linked...,
Is the thread of contact I am determined to keep open!
And is the reason why you will never defeat me...,
Christ is my first loyalty!

Let us start from the premise,
That I am easily aware of your condition...,
Your boasting that you have placed all employees that surround you,
Seems more to me of a curse than a blessing...,
And may ultimately have given you away!

My second loyalty is to my family,
Whose values are my responsibility!
My third loyalty is to my country,
As long as it maintains the values of the Creator!
My next loyalty is to them that pay me, if they accept my order of loyalty?

I am naturally concerned with increase,
So I must out of kindness voice my priorities...,
Which I imagine does not coincide with your comfort,
I will stay, or I will go, but I will not submit to an empty vessel....
Like Christ, I am your redeemer, or your judgment!

Chapter 108

The Rod of Iron

THE increase of "Trinities' Flame" presses into the crowd. Gain becomes apparent, albeit, some of them wonder why they begin to feel so unsettled.

Shakespeare said,

"This above all, to *thine* own *self* be true!"

To discover this..., all the rest becomes secondary, and of consequence. I used to sacrifice *"Increase"* in order to accommodate the limited, however, I became limited. I used to sacrifice *"Comfort"* in order to comfort others, nonetheless, I became discomforted. I used to deny *"Self"* in order to accept others. Even so, I went unaccepted. I would repeatedly allow myself to be pulled back through the eye of the needle, in order to fit in..., yet, nothing fit....

Not to mention the awkward perceptions thus created....

> Everyone becomes a villain!
> Everyone is plotting against you!
> Everyone wants a part of you!

The reality is, since you have relinquished your *"Increase,"* your *"Comfort,"* and your *"Self,"* you have also unwittingly relinquished your *"Power,"* in order to fit in, and that is why nothing will fit.

In your attempt to fit in, you have at the same time, allowed yourself to be dominated by those of the world, and now you appear to be the villain, because you are no longer being true to your own *"Self!"*

"To *thine* own *self* be true," means to disregard externals, and external perceptions, and to surrender everything outside of yourself to its own device. That which will be lifted..., will be lifted! That which won't be lifted..., won't be lifted! It is all in God's hands.

When I appeased them, I was just another voice in the crowd, and my words carried little weight, even when speaking the truth.

But when I am true to the Christ within, I am a voice above the crowd, my words carry weight, and the Christ presence demands to be heard....

By allowing those of the world the upper hand, they are able to usurp your authority and power, and place themselves between you and your "Divine Presence." Thus, setting themselves up as gods....

The Lord's fiat states that, "there is only one God, and there shall be no other god's before him." By allowing Christ the upper hand, he is the "Authority and the Power" to be dealt with, and who shall question such authority? Surrender all authority to the Christ within so that He may be second to none..., and you will have remained loyal and true to your "*True Self.*" In this way, the "Scepter of Authority" will be passed to us!

Chapter 109

The Wellspring

NOW seems like as good a time as any,
To express this forceful state of affairs!
The sheer extent of the subtle exchanges of energy,
That occur between one another is overwhelming...,
The law that governs the flow of energy and water are one....

It is natural that water flows,
To its lowest source without recourse to blame!
Yet, in a person the principle flows,
And everyone appears guilty...,
Though I am certain and hopeful...,
That with the proper handling of this crisis,
Will be born permanent fruits of attainment....
If I dam up the source, I feel well,
But others seem undernourished....
If I allow the source to flow freely,
Then I become the empty cup....
And it never fails that the few,
Who draw the most from your well, come to expect it,
And soon take on a sinister appearance...,
Or, are they actual tools of the sinister force...?
Is it proper to attempt to judge?
Who should receive and who should not?
And then if so, well how much?
This is precisely where I stand...,
This is my cross to bear!

Who are the truly sinister?
Whom do I mistake to be sinister?
Or, is everyone benevolent...,
And turned into coffins and death vaults by my twisted suspicion?
But I know better than that!

Chapter 110

THE MORNING STAR

WHAT would the possibility be...?
If one wanted to test the identity,
Of an upcoming star,
By placing him in the midst,
Of numerous ones which,
Lack primarily identity, in want of integrity...?

It is without question a fact,
That the integrated one,
Would be pressed upon immensely,
Forced to do one of two things....
He would have to gather his resources,
Organize his self and stay centered,

To maintain center, he would have to go slow,
Not allowing his self to be pushed, pressured, or oppressed....
If he did not gather his resources,
He would become easy prey for disorder....
Disorder would replace harmony,
And he would lose center,

To lose center is to lose one's identity,
Swallowed up in a whirlpool of nonessentials....
Could it be a possibility, that identity is being tested?
Alone in the midst of elemental turbulence,
To see if this star can maintain itself!
What would the possibility be...?

Chapter 111

THE KING OF KINGS

IN the beginning, the spirit of God moved upon the face of the deep. The deep itself became the first firmament of creation, and God called it heaven. This first firmament is of spirit.

And the unformed God said, let there be orbs within the firmament of heaven that shall be for habitations for all that shall proceed out of me, that is of spirit. Thus, the "Heavenly Kingdom" was established, and God saw that it was good.

And the spirit of God said, let there be a second firmament of creation for all that shall proceed out of me, and God called it earth. This second firmament is of matter.

And God said let the earth be for habitations for all that shall proceed out of me that is of matter. Thus, the "Earthly Kingdom" was established, and God saw that it was good.

And the spirit of God said, let there be a partition between the firmaments, between the heaven and the earth, and between me and all that shall proceed out of me, to preserve sanctity. Let it divide spirit from matter, night from day, and timelessness from time, and God saw that it was good.

And the yet unformed God said, let there be minerals within the orbs and planets of both firmaments, so that they will be enriched, and they were placed on the side of spirit, and on the side of matter. Thus, the "Mineral Kingdom" was established, and God saw that it was good.

And again, the unformed God said, let there be seed of all kinds sprinkled upon the orbs and planets of both firmaments, that shall bring forth fruit bearing trees, herb bearing plants and vines, and grasses and grains of all kinds, so that they will be bountiful, and they were placed on the side of spirit, and on the side of matter. Thus, the "Vegetable Kingdom" was established, and God saw that it was good.

When the spirit of God looked upon his creation and saw that it was good, he said, let there be life-producing organisms, and gene-bearing beasts of beauty, resource and splendor on both sides of the firmament that shall produce after their kind so as to produce diversity, pedigree and striving, let them be for food, shelter and work, and they were placed on the side of spirit, and on the side of matter. Thus, the life-producing organisms and the circle of animals were created, the "Animal Kingdom" was established, and God saw that it was good.

When the unformed God imagined the perfect vehicle in which to manifest his self in form on both sides of the firmament, he set out to devise a magnificent, terrestrial yet transcendent means of expression, utilizing the utmost in imagination, design, functionality, insight and wisdom. He perfected this image in his mind and decided to call it "Man," and he saw that it was very good.

One morning, in a brilliant flash of creativity and spontaneity, the unformed God became his perfect thought form, in that quantum moment in the heavens! Thus, the divine image of "Man" was created! The "Godly Kingdom" was established, and God saw that it was very good.

Over time, the formed yet unformed God, thought into being, untold bands of companions, friends and servants to do his bidding, made in his own image and endowed with supernatural beauty, purpose, power and authority, yet a little bit removed from the supremacy of the Godhead, and the deity decided to call them "Angels." Thus, the "Angelic Kingdom" was established, and God saw that it was good.

After yet awhile, the Godhead decided to bring forth others, children and offspring, made in his own image, that they may call him Father. He wanted to endow them with all the beauty, purpose, power and authority of the angels but without the supernatural qualities, so he made them a little lower than the angels. Thus, God created his first male child and called him Adam. Then God created his first female child and called her Eve, and he decided to call them "Human." So, Adam and Eve were created on the heavenly side of the firmament. God wanted his children to be the pinnacle of beauty, creativity, potential and love. God loved his children who were made in his own image, and so he charged his angels to watch over them. Thus, the "Human Kingdom" was established, and God saw that it was good.

Thus, the divine image of "Man" and all of the "Kingdoms" were established in the heavens, in a place the deity called Eden, and God saw that it was good.

In time, God the Father determined that in order for his human children to reach and fulfill their God given "Potential," they would have to leave their heavenly Eden, become living souls, becoming earthbound, and sojourn upon a terrestrial Eden in order to partake of the "Tree of Knowledge," and its fruit of "Good and Evil!"

Thus, God left the firmament of heaven and came to his pearl of planets, earth, which he named earthly Eden," as an extension of the heavenly Eden. He brought forth his first male child Adam from the dust of the ground, and breathed life into him and Adam became a living soul, becoming earthbound. He caused a deep sleep to come over him, and removed one of his ribs and laid it on the ground, then he brought forth his first female child Eve from the dust of the ground, and breathed life into her and Eve became a living soul, becoming earthbound.

God brought the beasts of the field to Adam and Eve, and instructed them to name them, and to take dominion over them. He commanded the beasts of the field to serve Adam and Eve and their seed, and the animals understood, and God saw that it was good.

And the Lord God walked with Adam and Eve amidst the garden of earthly Eden. They talked, and God shared his visions with them of his "Human" family, and of a bountiful earth. They walked in the cool of the evening and Adam and Eve asked many questions of the Lord, and they called him "Father."

The Lord God took Adam and Eve to the middle of the garden, and showed them the "Tree of Knowledge," and explained to them that of all the trees in the garden, this one yields the fruit of "Good and Evil," and he said, of all the trees of the garden, thou mayest freely eat, but of this tree, thou mayest not eat, for in the day that ye eat, ye shall surely die! And the Lord God looked at Adam and Eve, and they understood, and they continued to walk, away from the tree in the midst of the garden.

The Lord God kissed Adam and Eve each one, and blessed them, and said, be fruitful and multiply, and fulfill my vision. Then the Lord God turned away and left them, he walked and he was not. Adam and Eve looked at each other awestruck, with gaping mouths, they stood there alone, in the midst of the garden of earthly Eden, in the cool of the evening, in all their glorious nakedness, and they knew it not.

The formed yet unformed God in his infinite wisdom foresaw the need to protect his earthly children upon the earthly Eden, and again, charged his angels to watch over them, hence, the angels became the "Watchers," and God saw that it was good.

After some time again, there was a rift in heaven…. God's first created angel and pinnacle of his "Angelic" creation became of the mind, that God the Father, had a more "majestic and transcendent" plan for his "Human Kingdom" than he did for his "Angelic Kingdom," and that God, after having created the angels first, and after having companioned with them longer, must ultimately cherish and love his "Human" creation more than the "Angelic." After all, the "Angelic" was created a little higher than the "Human" and they were supernatural beings, endowed with greater beauty, purpose, power and authority."

Thus, Lucifer, the "Sun of the Morning," and a third of his angels rebelled against God the Father and his angels. The rebellion became an uprising, Archangel Michael fought and his angels, and Lucifer fought and his angels, and Lucifer and a third of his angels were banished from heaven, neither was their place found anymore in heaven…. Thus, Lucifer and his "Bands of Angels" had fallen from grace, they had fallen from the "Most High" and the heavens, and they became known as the "Fallen Angels."

The "Fallen Angels" decided to make war with God's "Human Kingdom" on earth. They would exact their "Angelic Rage" upon his "Human" children, and upon his earthly Eden….

The "Fallen Angels" decided it fit to take to themselves, the women of earthly Eden, not that they were fairer than the "Angelic," but to make them less "Human" and more "Supernatural," and their offspring became known as the "Nephilim."

Thus, by corrupting the original "Genetic Code" of God's "Human Kingdom," the "Fallen Angels" thwarted his "Divine Plan" by interfering with the "True Humans."

God, being God, full of infinite wisdom, would redeem his "Human Kingdom," he would devise a mission, and send a "Messenger" to reclaim and restore what was rightfully his. He would send "Himself" in the form of his "Son," to redeem his "True Human" children. He would now create the pinnacle of pinnacles of all of his kingdoms.... His "Only Begotten Son" full of grace and truth and majesty. His "Son" would be called the "Christ," and he would be born "Under the Law," in order to be the "Law," so that those who believe on him, and on him who sent him, may be redeemed and reclaim their "Divine" inheritance. He would construct a being that would be a representation of him, endowed with the "Divine" grace, wisdom, power and authority adequate to the task of saving his "Human" creation.

This being would naturally be gifted with the anointing of the Father because they would be "One" in essence. This "Only Begotten Son" of God would be his representative on earth. His "Christ" would be his "Messenger" to earth. This agent of the "Christ" would be the intermediary between the firmaments, between the "Heavens and the Earth," between "All That Is, and the Human Race" sojourning in earthly Eden.

The person of the "Christ," being the manifestation of God himself, by being the first, finest and most magnificent of God's creations fashioned after his own self, and above all others, became in essence, his first born "Son!" Therefore, he is the first, and since there shall be no other God, he is the last..., hence the name, "Alpha and Omega," the first and the last! This "Son" now has many names, counselor, teacher, prince of peace, the great physician, not the least of which is known as the "King of Kings!"

Thus, Christ is the manifestation of God wherever he happens to be. He is appointed to return at intervals as the "Victory" of life over death! As the "Messenger" of God, and as the "Incarnation of the Word," thus, to "Judge" the living and the dead....

Jesus said that he and his Father are "One," therefore, they are synonymous by "Divine Nature," the magnificence of each inherent within the other. Make no mistake about it, Jesus is the prophesied Christ, he is the "Lamb of God" who was made flesh, slain and sacrificed for the sake of God's "Human Kingdom!" He is the prophesied "One," and there shall be no other. For those of mankind who refuse to acknowledge Him as the "Son of God" that he is, while insisting on waiting for the next messiah to come along, shall be greatly disappointed..., and the "True Messiah" will not recognize any who have failed to recognize him, for God will not be mocked!

The "King of Kings" also continually exudes perfect love, wisdom and power as part of his "Divine" nature, which are his central bonding qualities. The widely held beliefs that God and his Son can hold families, groups and nations together, does not go unfounded, They, the Godhead, are the underlying principle of integration.

When Jesus commanded wind and wave to be at peace, he was exercising his dominion over the elements, that is, of the atoms and molecules themselves, even as the "Almighty" holds galaxies and solar systems together, and sustains orbits of planets revolving around their stars.

The person of the Christ, likewise, holds these selfsame qualities of attraction, cohesion and magnetism resident within his being, giving him the ability to literally "Hold the Elements" together, while simultaneously maintaining dominion over them. Thus, Christ, the "King of Kings" is integration in action wherever he is present. Just as equally as those who deny the existence of God, and his Son, cannot help things from falling apart, from disintegrating. Jesus demonstrated this when he walked on water to test Peter's faith, the mere outstretch of his hand was sufficient to raise Peter, regardless of his lack of faith.

This profound and transcendent application of the "Holy Science," or "Miracle" to be exact, is not peculiar to the "Son of God." It is part and parcel of his being. A truly spiritual being is also "Wholly Scientific," for there has never been a separation between science and spirit, except in the mind of man!

Thus, God's mission to redeem his "Human Kingdom" has been accomplished through his Son Jesus the Christ. Jesus the "Messiah" of mankind became the "Messenger" of God in his earthly incarnation when he walked the streets of Galilee two millennia ago.

Since that time, there have been multitudes of "True Israelites" and "True Believers" who have followed Christ in the regeneration. Millions have sought and accepted him, and thus, have been redeemed from the foundation of the earth. Those whose names have been added to the "Book of Life," are among the first fruits of God's "Human Kingdom!" These are among the Overcomers who will follow Christ into the "New Jerusalem!"

And now a word of inspiration for the Overcomers..., a few words describing the "Exceeding Great Promises," promised them in the "*Holy Bible,*" that they shall receive upon entering into the "New Jerusalem!"

The "New Jerusalem" will be built upon a "New Earth!" The "New Earth" will be on another "Dimension" than this earth.... The "New Earth" will be as "Heaven" to those who live there, thus, there will be a "New Heaven" and a "New Earth!"

The Overcomers will undergo a process of rebirth and reunification. Each one will be re-created in their original image, and in their original essence. Their original God given "Genetic Code" will be restored to each one..., they will each be refashioned into their peak of youth, beauty and perfection..., and this will be an "Eternal Transformation!"

At that time, once transformation is complete, they will go through a process of reunification.... Each one will be rejoined with their true "Dyadic Mate," which is their "Divine Counterpart" and "Other Half," which is also their true "Twin" or "Soul Mate!" As the "Twins" become "One" in the eternal embrace of reunification, they will together begin a new evolutionary journey as immortal couples, and heirs of Christ in the macrocosmic self, or "Body of God!" These "Twins" will each be a permanent "Locus of Identity and Individuation" of the Creator..., with each providing vital and specialized services and functions to the Creation.... As there is no superfluity within the "Universal Grid," each will have a role to play..., and they shall no more go out....

There will be joy unceasing and wonders to behold..., there will be love and expression, there will be travel and adventure, there will be family and friends, all on a "New Earth" and under a "New Heaven," created at the height of perfection and beyond means of expression....

Each "Twin" couple will be given their own estate, their fertile lands and endowments, their vineyards, their farms and fields, their herds and flocks and beasts. But there will no longer be work as you know it. There will be living, at its zenith.... There will no longer be weight on your backs, or sweat on your brows..., there will be exploration, and discovery, of yourselves and God's Creation in the "Eternal Moment" in which you find yourselves.... Forever!

Chapter 112

The Twelve Tribes of Israel

THE children of Israel are the descendants of Isaac. The children of Ishmael are the descendants of Ishmael. Both Isaac and Ishmael are the descendants of Abraham. Ishmael was Abraham's first born son, Isaac was Abraham's second born son.

Abraham chose his second born son Isaac to be the rightful heir of his seed, and so the children of Isaac became the rightful inheritors. Isaac had two sons, Esau and Jacob, but Esau despised his birthright, and sold it to Jacob for a pottage of lentils and bread. So Jacob became the sole inheritor of the seed of Isaac. Jacob was renamed Israel after wrestling with an angel of the Lord, and he had twelve sons, they were...,

---

Reuben
The firstborn! The dignified and powerful, but unstable as water!

Simeon and Levi
The instruments of cruelty and wrath, they slew a man!

Judah
The Lion of Israel! He who will carry "the Scepter of the Twelve Tribes" Until Shiloh comes, (the New Jerusalem), "he shall gather the people Together at the end," prior to the coming of (the New Jerusalem), "The Lawgiver," the one whom the brothers will praise!

Zebulun
The seafarer and fisherman!

Issachar
The strong, the worker of the fields!

Dan
The judge of Israel, and cunning like the serpent!

Gad
The oppressed, but he will overcome in the end!

ASHER
The lover of fine things!

NAPHTALI
The hind of the brothers, the eloquent with words!

JOSEPH
The Strength of the Lord! "The Warrior who was sorely grieved by the Archers," The stone of Israel, "the shepherd who held the tribes together," He who will be blessed!

BENJAMIN
The ravenous wolf, he who gathers the spoils!

These twelve sons of Jacob are the progenitors of "*the Twelve Tribes of the Children of Israel*," who today comprise the Jewish people, and the Jewish nation, but are not confined to these. Most importantly, they are the progenitors of the "True Israelites" and the "True Believers!"

One must take into account, the fact that there are only two roots, in regard to the "Twelve Tribes," and only two branches, yet the world today consists of billions of people and many nations and races, therefore, one must accept that the "Transmigration of Souls," the Bible's terminology for the process of re-embodiment, has resulted in the relocation and re-nationalization of the multitudes of the descendants of the children of Israel, as well as the descendants of the children of Ishmael.

Abraham sent his first born son Ishmael away, who was not the chosen heir of his seed, and so the children of Ishmael were not the chosen inheritors of the seed of Abraham. The children of Ishmael today comprise the Arab people, and the Arab nations, but are not confined to these. Due to the "Transmigration of Souls," there are multitudes of the descendants of Ishmael who have likewise undergone the process of relocation and re-nationalization since the day of Abraham. And consequently, many have joined the ranks of the "True Israelites" and "True Believers" through the path of belief, acceptance, and conversion, in the "Son of God," in "God the Father," and in the "Holy Spirit!"

Chapter 113

The Israelites and the Philistines

THE world is divided into two camps. On the one hand we have those who have accepted God and his Son, and on the other hand we have those who have denied God and his Son. Those who have accepted, and believe in God have life, while those who have denied, and disbelieve in God do not have life. The "True Believers" are the remnant of the "Twelve Tribes," the disbelievers are the Philistines. The remnant, are the "True Israelites," while the Philistines are the smug atheists. The "haves" are in one camp, the "have nots" are in the other.... For this reason, we say the haves and the have nots....

"He that hath the Son hath life;
And he that hath not the Son of God hath not life."

- 1 John 5: 12

The Philistines are those who have warred against the "True Israelites" from the very beginning, and throughout the ages, thus, the seed of the "Philistine Type" originated upon the corruption of God's "Human Kingdom" by the "Fallen Angels" when they were cast out of heaven. These corruptors have since infiltrated the four corners of the earth.

The Philistines today, may come from any race or place of origin. They are not confined to a nation, or to any group of nations, although some nations have more disbelievers than believers.... They do not belong to any one creed or club. They are not confined to any particular social stratum. They are the rich and poor alike. They are the political, and apolitical. They are the powerless, and the powerful. Some have agendas and goals, some do not. Some have religious objectives, some have economic ones. Some target religion, some target profits. Some seek to annihilate, others seek to overpower....

However, their denial of Christ, and subsequently of God, has ultimately severed them from life itself. They have unwittingly cut themselves off from the parent vine and fount of eternal life, and have thus sealed their fates....

The have nots often rise to great seats of influence and prominence in the world because they are of the world. They find it easy to achieve their ends because they have no spiritual values to compromise, or any morals or principalities to wrestle with. Darwin's theory on the "Survival of the Fittest," is among their philosophies.... These are the very ones who continually seek to find a "Missing Link" between the "Animal Kingdom" and the "Human Kingdom!" But, in vain, will they search for something that does not exist....

In order to set the record straight, the truth must be told, for the "Truth" will out.... The "Genetic Code" of the "True Human" as God had created him, has not only been corrupted by the seed of the "Fallen Angels," resulting in "Nephilim" offspring..., it has also been desecrated and manipulated by its co-mingling with the DNA of some higher primates on the planet..., resulting in, a hybridization of certain primates in the "Animal Kingdom," and an abomination of certain humans in the "Human Kingdom."

Thus, the "True Human" is a product of "Divine Creation" stemming from the "Human Kingdom" from God's Heavenly Eden. The "True Primate" is a product of "Divine Creation" stemming from the "Animal Kingdom" from God's earthly Eden. Thus, the "Human" is human; the "Animal" is animal.... They were each created distinct and separate from each other, thus, the "Kingdoms" were created.

Now, it is only "Man" in his unnatural mind, and unspiritual ways that seeks in vain to combine the two into a Godless, evolutionary herd, predominantly led by the "Animal!" There is no "Missing Link!" There never has been! The only "Missing Link" that exists is a "Spiritual One" from your hierarchical chain of divinity.... Alternatively, it is the only one that can be found!

Henceforth,

>Let the "Genetic Code" of the "True Human"
>Be removed from the "Animal!"

>Let the "Genetic Code" of the "Animal"
>Be removed from the "True Human!"

And let each one receive its original and rightful "Genetic Code!"

- Selah

The "True Israelites" are those who have been sustained by the fount of living water. They have been given the "Gift of Life," and they are infinitely more durable, as water wears away the rock.... They are the laborers in the fields..., they are the people in the streets..., and they are the husband and wife struggling to make ends meet.... They are those without status or credit in the world, they are the discredited, sometimes they are the down and out, the social outcasts who are being chastened by the Lord....

"As many as I love, I rebuke and chasten:
Be zealous therefore, and repent."

- Revelation 3: 19

Meanwhile, these "Robbers of God" take what is not given to them. Their browsing and shopping and artful dodging is not so much shopping as stealing, the "Grace of God" from the holy innocents. They lust after those who have life....

The Philistines likewise sit in powerful seats in high places, in exclusive groups and governments, in corporations and trusts, in royalty and familial blood, passed on from generation to generation, and wickedly scheming the execution of complete world domination...

Which agenda to push..., which action to take?
Which lie to devise..., which propaganda to slake?

Which truth to malign..., which value to decry?
Which politician to back..., which hero to sack?

Which threat to impose..., which right to take?
Which crony to stack..., which neck to hack?

Which goods to exploit..., which shortage to fake?
Which boycott to levy..., which story to shape?

Which villain to make..., which reserve to take?
Which punishment to exact..., which country to break?

Of course, the players at this level of the global game are the few, the super rich, the controlling power elite, the aristocracy. They are the few who own the resources..., they are the ones who manage the wealth..., they are the ones who have an agenda..., they are the ones who wage war for the sake of controlling the resources, and maintaining the power. They are the ones who have committed untold acts of tyranny and atrocity in their quest to subjugate and enslave the masses and the just....

They are the ones who have torched the saints! They are the ones who have beheaded the prophets! They are the ones who have crucified the Christ! They are the ones who have slain the "martyrs," and the "Holy Innocents" from time immemorial, against which the "martyrs" have cried....

Well, take heed, oh Philistines, the "Day of Judgment" has come!

Chapter 114

The Burning Cell

ONE last thing concerning the have nots! It suddenly becomes obvious who the ones are that are championing Darwin's theory of evolution....

Clearly, after denying the existence of a benign benefactor such as the "Almighty," one stands bereft of that support. Belief, acceptance and faith in a "Divine Being" is the root of that support, and without it, one can only wither away, and the withered branch will soon be cut off....

These being the condition, these unbelievers and "Robbers of God" have only one direction in which to go. They do their best to group together and further their agenda. An agenda that would in essence, remove the root of their problem from schools, institutions, and from society at large.

The problem with their agenda is not only that it is ungodly, but that it actually causes people to live in sin, to propagate sin, and to accept sin as a way of life, in ways that they would otherwise not, were these ways not legalized and incorporated into the very fabric of our lives....

These laws that justify sin continue to erode the standards of "Right Living." They undermine the "Values" of the good and just. They blaspheme the institution of "Holy Matrimony" between a husband and a wife. They corrupt the "Morals" of youth and children. It is no less than a battle of good against evil that is being waged here!

They stand in arrogant defiance of the "Law of the One." They insist out of fear, their separation from the Creator. They see themselves as separate from God, His Creation, and from all that is, in the stance of the true existentialist....

The Bible calls them the *fearful!*

They band together to fight in the courts of law to remove God from His own Creation! They protest and bring class action suits against the government in order to rid our schools, institutions and courthouses of "God's Commandments." They rally against any public display of the "Cross." They are offended that "Christmas" contains the word Christ, denying the fact of the "Redeemer's" birth..., citing it an offense to their religious affiliation. Hypocrites! All mind you, under the justification of the separation of church and state....

The Bible calls them *unbelievers!*

They organize to legislate and establish the right of homosexual and lesbian marriage, in the name of equal rights....

The Bible calls it *abomination!*

They fight to preserve the right to terminate the life of the unborn, under the guise of a woman's right to choose....
The Bible calls it *murder*!

They demand the right to produce, sell, and display sex, pornography and lasciviousness in their stores, and on their websites, under the pretense of free expression....
The Bible calls it sin and *whoremongering*!

They sell the latest edition of children's books, to fill their hearts and minds with fantastical tales of witchcraft and spells, they even offer formulas for the young apprentice, and the parents are the first in line..., under the cover of literary exercise....
The Bible calls it *sorcery*!

They puncture and riddle their bodies to decorate them with cheap ornaments, and an endless barrage of tattoos, icons and images, which only serve to defile and desecrate their temples, in the ruse of individuality....
The Bible calls it *idolatry*!

They conjure up fable and folklore and combine it with some enigmatic quirks of a brilliant man in order to propagate a lie, and plant the seeds of disbelief in the minds of the people, all by way of speculation....
The Bible calls it *lies*!

> "But the fearful, and unbelieving, and the abominable, and murderers,
> And whoremongers, and sorcerers, and idolaters, and all liars,
> Shall have their part in the lake which burneth with fire
> And brimstone: which is the second death."
>
> - Revelation 21: 8

Woe to the *fearful*! Woe to all those who have fallen for the first lie! Woe to all those who see themselves as separate from the Creator, and hence from His Creation! Fear is a cardinal sin! "Man" was created to be the "Steward" of the earth. He was designed to take "Dominion" over the earth and walk in full conscious unity with the Creator. But man fell for the first untruth! The untruth that told him he was separate from his Creator. Once "Man" saw himself as apart and separate from God, he succumbed to fear, and has been living in fear ever since! I've got bad news for you! The source of your feelings of dread and anguish is not your existentialist nature, it is the fear that you embraced....

Woe to all *unbelievers*! Woe to all who fight to remove God from His own Creation! Woe to those who would deny their own maker! The smug atheists have always been the true Philistines. Unbelief is a cardinal sin! It involves a being, who has been given the "Gift of Life," yet that being has continually denied, and refuted his or her most essential part that is required for their existence!

They are like orphaned children who have denied their own Father. They are like reeds swaying in the winds, which have denied their own roots. I've got bad news for you! If you have fought to remove God from His own Creation, God will remove you from His Creation! And there will be no courts of appeal for you to petition! The separation of church and state is a convention of "Man," and not a "Divine Injunction!" If you are offended by the "Son of Man," or by his title of Christ, you will be an offense to Him when He comes into His "Kingdom!"

Woe to all *abominations*! Woe to all those who are an abomination in God's eyes! Woe to those who have been judged a defiler of God's Creation! I've got bad news for you! If you are considered an abomination in the eyes of the "Lord of Creation," it is a travesty to think that you have any rights at all...! Hear what I am saying! If you have been judged and found to be an abomination in God's eyes, "you have no rights," they all have been taken away...!

Woe to all *murderers*! Woe to the murderers of God's children! Woe to the murderers of the womb! I've got bad news for you! "Man is not the origin of life, nor is he the ender of life!" That has and always will be God's jurisdiction, and you have treaded upon "Sacred Ground...!"

Woe to all *whoremongers*! Woe to all those who sell their bodies for a profit! Woe to all those who defile the innocent to become wealthy! I've got bad news for you! Just the names of two cities that might jog your memories, "Sodom and Gomorrah...!"

Woe to all *sorcerers*! Woe to all wizards and witches! Woe to all those who corrupt the hearts and minds of the innocent at a profit! Woe to all those who use the black arts! Woe to all those who have used, and will use the black arts at the hands of their unwitting subjects! I've got bad news for you! "Henceforth, whatever measure is meted out by a practitioner of the black arts that selfsame measure will be meted out to him or her fourfold, hence, from the four quarters of the earth it shall return to them even unto their own destruction.... Selah!"

Woe to all *idolaters*! Woe to all the desecrators of God's temples! Woe to all those who defile the body for the sake of an image, or a look! Is your hatred so great that you have unleashed it upon yourselves? I've got bad news for you! The "Bodies of Man" are the "Temples of God" that have been loaned to you, the ones that you have made foul...!

Woe to all *liars*! Woe to all those who pervert the truth or cast shadows of doubt on the truth for a profit or otherwise! Woe to those who lie in order to cover up sin! I've got bad news for you! "Henceforth, your lie shall be counted as two!" Woe to all liars who call themselves priests, and pastors, and reverends and such, for if your vocation is to guide people in spiritual principle, "henceforth, your lies will be your undoing, even until you are unfrocked!"

If Christ had fathered a child, then that would have been "Divinely Ordained" and part of his mission. If the seed of Christ came to reside in France, then France would have been the "Promised Land! The significance of the blood of Christ is a spiritual matter, not a physical one. In regard to the Merovingian line, none have ever had the blood of Christ except those who have partaken of the "Body and Blood" of Christ, and have been converted and "Born Again," just as everyone else in the "Human Race!"

Thus, the "Law" has been given, and "Justice" has been served. Let it be known to all beforehand, that any ill will, or ill intent, or attempts of desecration against "My Messenger" or "His Image," will invoke a swift and appropriate response by his "Angelic Guard," the "Archangels," and even from "I the Father!" No further warning will be issued!

Henceforth,

"From the four corners of the earth is he defended,
And from both sides of the firmament is he watched and preserved!"

- Selah

America the great was the "Promised Land." Its constitution, its "Bill of Rights," and the government itself, was conceived and founded upon by the tenets and teachings of the "*Holy Bible*." The word of God was interpreted by "Just Stewards" of the law and it became the foundation of the United States of America. Its laws are not perfect, for the laws of all nations are the creation and convention of "Man," and no law should ban the "Creator from His own Creation!" Today, that covenant has been broken. The agendas of the have nots, the Philistines and "Robbers of God" have succeeded. In order to save America, and in turn the planet as a whole, that covenant has to be restored, and it has to be restored by "Man." America cannot long stand without the backing of the Creator. God and his precepts must be brought back into our hearts and lives, back into our families, our cities and nations. Otherwise, it will be too late....

So you see, the have nots have nothing to lose, but they do have an aim. That aim is to tear down and destroy this great bastion of freedom that God has so amply provided. These are the final revengeful attempts of desecration against the "Almighty" and his "Human Kingdom," right here in America, by an envious, vacant diminishing race!

Chapter 115

The Persecution

THIS I pass on to the very few,
The question of what to do...,
Concerning "increase" and "decrease,"
To those vowed to embody eternal truth...,
And walk the earth as Christ!

Give no quarter!
Compromise no needless time!
Allow no bleeding heart!
Never allow thy portion to diminish...,
Out of pity for their uncomfortable-ness!
Even justified pity...,
Of their desperate state,
Will be siphoned to your detriment....
Do not hate, evaluate...,
It is God's substance they take!
It is very simple...,
Forfeit your victory to appease the Herods,
And they will offer you anything...,
Or accumulate your weight in light,
And win the round!
We may be meek...,
But Christ won't be pushed around,
We may be light, but we are not lightweight...,
Unable to win, they begin to accuse...,
And plot to disorganize you!

But fret not, for you are persecuted for Christ's sake,
And are indeed the winner!
You see, Christ has always been the winner...,
And they have always been the losers...,
So they sulk, and accuse, and persecute the "Holy Infants!"

Chapter 116

The Crucifixion

IF you would bear the burden of Christ!
You must be willing to embrace loneliness,
Every step closer you come to your Christ self,
Is a step away from the worldly minded!

As you follow the injunction to come up higher...,
The distance from the worldly minded increases,
This vibratory distance is definitely felt, though misunderstood,
To those yet engaged in the world's momentums....

The misunderstanding between vibratory levels...,
Leads to an inner separation between individuals,
Once inner separation occurs,
Outer separation naturally follows....

Since Christ is "One" in essence with all life...,
Who is it that causes this separation?
It is the one, who senses himself,
Outside of the circle of holiness....

It becomes imperative...,
To earn your daily bread amongst the "Anointed,"
This is what it means to be crucified in matter...,
Which you must be willing and able to endure, joyfully!

Chapter 117

THE FLAME

UNTIL you internalize a just portion of your Christhood,
You do not fully experience the changing of the seasons....
Until the fire within equals or surpasses the fire without,
The revolving scenery is mainly an external event....

Oh..., but to feel the fire inside, that is living!

After winter's convalescence,
The kindling fires of spring,
Warms and reaches new heights!

Tender blossoms of youth...,
Explode into summer,
Realizing Buddha's nature!

And on, into autumns solemn wonder...,
Each rose hangs on to the end..., midst winds twirling,
And leaves burning, each rose dies a gentle death!

Chapter 118

THE first day of summer is here,
Again, I have not adhered,
To God, His precepts, the laws!
My own worst enemy is myself!

I feel cut off, detached, solo,
The line of communication put on hold,
Suspended, in a less integrated world...,
I have misqualified once too often!

I have tested the patience of the "Presence,"
Forced His mercy to be withdrawn,
His chastening and rebuke withheld...,
I have distanced myself from Him!

Last night as I slept, my soul soared,
Well over brown barren ground and darkness,
Not a single sign of life around...,
Nor mood, emotion, or virtue found!

Chapter 119

The Sorrow

WISH I could cry out more heartily for redemption,
A wail from the gut of existence,
That trembles the web of life...,
My will and I have grown somber!

The strength it involves to inspire hope,
Must be better spent on daily tasks,
Surrounded on four sides by debts I owe...,
Will not keep me from deserting the marketplace!

I have dashed all familial expectations,
Of becoming an ambitious, productive son,
In hope to serve God, yet I am the one...,
Who hinders, halts, and ruins, the gifts that I've won!

It has been said before so truthfully, I too must reiterate the experience,
That God can rescue us from all manner of cataclysm,
And even from the snares of the Devil...,
But he cannot save us from ourselves!

Chapter 120

The Breath of Life

I REMEMBER when life was full of joy and newfound wonder. Innocence was the key. Priority played little, and my decisions were based mainly on my likes and dislikes....

But for the spiritually inclined, everything becomes a matter of priority, and all decisions are based entirely upon necessity....

Everything unnecessary becomes burdensome, weighty, and is bought with a price. One's life is thereby reduced to those activities and routines that have been tried and proven to be of benefit to what is primarily, "Life Inducing, Life Enhancing, and even Life Preserving." Thus, everything becomes a matter of "Value and Determination."

At the same time, it becomes convincingly clear which activities and behaviors must be omitted and left behind..., the mannerisms and mindsets that are deemed "Normal" and "Harmless" to those living in the world, have now become the old habitual patterns of living and thinking that engender the downward path and snuff out the "Spiritual Spark." The old ways have served their purpose, and are now known to be harmful to one's "Inner Man," to one's "Temple" in the making, which is one's "Holy Grail."

The elimination of these downward tendencies will allow God the opportunity to breathe new life into that "Grail," and to animate us anew....

Contrarily, reduction is precisely the opposite of what takes place. Life is again full of joy and newfound wonder!

Chapter 121

The Resurrection

DEAR friends,
Allow me to share,
A few words with the living,
For life is returning to me...,
And I shall return it to thee!

I have suffered diminishing light,
From varied shades of hopelessness, grief and fright,
Darkness surrounds you, as people crowd you,
Could not escape the feeling...,
Of desperation's plight!

And I have had the privilege of walking in the light,
From rainbow rays of love, to fiery white,
Grace adorns you, as angels warn you,
With joy overflowing in buoyant life,
A son of God, immortal right!

Chapter 122

The Fallen Angels

OUT of the tombs,
The martyrs cry...,
Avenge our blood,
For this we've died!

Up from the streets,
The brothers shriek...,
Justice be done,
Assist the meek!

Deep in the womb,
The Fetus weeps...,
At life withdrawn,
Aborted heaps!

Through outer space,
The angels race...,
To rid the earth,
Of fallen waste!

CHAPTER 123

THE LAST ANTICHRISTS

THE last three antichrists,
With hate and revenge,
Have presented the earth,
Three periods of blight!

The letters of their names,
Equaling six six six...,
Assigned a death warrant,
Upon their birthrights!

All three vowed to wage war,
And rebel against God...,
By killing His people,
Their children to fright!

The first two, technique,
Was murder outright!
The third, more timid,
A sneak by night!

```
S   H   A
  T   I   R
    A   T   A
      L   L   F
        I   E   A
          N   R   T
```

A Soviet dictator!
A Nazi fascist!
And would you believe...,
A diplomat of terror!

Chapter 124

 The End of Days

LIKE a cosmic fireball it plunged,
Bound to the antiquated place,
The fate of Chernobyl...,
Set a boulder in motion,

Giving the town's inhabitants,
Wormwood as token...,
Unleashing the "Horsemen,"
And signaling, the "End of Days!"

The problem with a boulder,
Just like dominoes set on precarious lots,
I mean, the event that one is pushed...,
None can be stopped....

So Gorbachev makes a defensive posture,
Visits New York, shifts his karmic lot...,
Strolls through boutiques and bourgeoisie shops,
Hoping his fortune, the apple to rot....

But justice of heaven reverses the plot,
Announcement of quakes, Armenia is tossed...,
Pondering on the game he lost, a humbled chessman....
But we do commend you one thing Mikhail, glasnost!

Chapter 125

The False Prophet

REARED up with a silver spoon,
The Saudi child did play...,
Born in the lap of luxury,
The world would await his day!

He watched the slaughter of his Afghan brothers,
At the hands of the soviet regime,
He vowed to fight, out of compassion,
And joined the Mujahadeen!

America aided the Muslim guerillas,
As did the Saudis and Chinese,
With Bin Laden's help, the fighters succeeded,
Humiliating the Russian machine!

All told, a half million Afghans slain,
Over four million refugees retained...,
The war continued, but Russia refrained,
Bin Laden's group, Al Qaeda was trained!

As fate would have it, Bin Laden decided,
To retaliate against the West,
He would target the symbols of wealth and power,
Have suicide bombers strike the twin towers!

Raised in the midst of abundance and privilege,
The "False Prophet" has gone terribly astray...,
As he evades and hides from place to place,
The turbaned one awaits his day!

Chapter 126

The Battle of Armageddon

LET us not overlook...,
The final four potentials,
That are lining up nicely,
To meet at Megiddo!

Alas, the long prophesied quartet...,
The rise of the antichrist himself,
Alongside, two horns like a lamb,
And a beast, coming out of the earth!

```
V  B  M
 P  A  A
  U  S  B
   T  S  B
    I  A  A
     N  D  S
```

A prince of Gog!
A son of Magog!
And would you believe...,
A Hamas ideologue!

Lest we forget,
Each sweet needs a sour,
The leader of Iran,
Gets nuclear power!

The letters of his name,
Come to eighteen,
Or, six, and six, and six...,
The number of a man!

When the prince of Gog,
And the two horns like a lamb,
Come to the aid,
Of a targeted Iran,

Hell's fury is unleashed...,
Against the State of Israel,
Devastating the Holy City...,
And Armageddon begins!

Chapter 127

The Seven Headed Beast

WHETHER jealous and revengeful Marx,
Or Engels' bourgeois façade,
From satanic youths who monger power,
To Lenin, who murdered the czar!

Be it a mindless assassin like Stalin,
Or psychotic Hitler's perverted spies...,
From Mao Tse-Tung's little red book,
To Gorbachev's seductive lies!

The gentle flower of the soul,
Crushed 'neath the mechanical wheel...,
Reduces man to serve the tool,
Turning genius into the fool!

The oppressor has ever been the soulless state,
Totalitarian rule needs to monopolize...,
By eloquent preaching of a godless philosophy,
Maintain the "Beast" in multifaceted disguise!

Chapter 128

The Man and the Machine

PEOPLE are formed in the world's image,
Unquestionably mold, cold as ice...,
No wonder true values are derided,
Everyone programmed from cradle to grave!

As the vision of men is all but eroded,
The final antichrist will take his seat...,
Big brother commands, and then demands,
Everyone dance to the nihilistic beat!

No more artists, no loners, heaven forbid, no thinkers,
No more waves that endanger the hedonistic sea...,
Denounce them, defile them, expose them, exile them,
Soon all will be soldiers, and thought obsolete!

Chapter 129

The Flesh and Blood Hero

OBSESSIVE, compulsive, they label me plain,
How they yearn to categorize...,
As if with a term, my goals to obtain,
The hero's journey can't be classified!

Rigid, dogmatic, they spurt and exclaim,
Upon spiritual talk they immobilize...,
Return to the shallow, brief topic maintain,
Who among you can handle the burden of truth?

Selfish, individual, seeks only his claim,
How they next learn to undermine...,
The noble, the pure, the holy above them,
Their own selves to jeopardize!

"The little man, Reich says, wants only to serve,
The little big man," what little self worth....
In the end, it is the flesh and blood hero,
Who refuses to worship the soulless state!

Chapter 130

The Red Dragons of Death

INJUSTICE looms round every corner,
Alas, there is no refuge...,
Thieving have nots rigged computer,
Channeling astral deluge!

Hateful atheists bind and quarter,
Those who innocently love...,
Smile and lie, plot and devour,
Man-children's comfort dove!

Truth less, heartless, dragons of death,
Set snares that can't be seen...,
Feign love you, help you, never distress you,
Entangle you in their dream!

Judgment day sounds of awesome wonder,
The dead without Christ are dust...,
Horses of angels draw chariots of thunder,
To locate and judge, cancel out the unjust!

Chapter 131

The Four Horsemen of the Apocalypse

THE hour of the "Horsemen" is upon us,
There is no room left for peace...,
People's days are full and empty,
While they are ill at ease!

Their work time is an affliction,
Their free time an addiction...,
Their full time search for fun and action,
Allows part time satisfaction!

Their values speak, don't worry be happy,
Their morals reek, their virtues nappy...,
They say you live once, life's a party,
He's too serious, quite foolhardy!

Their vision extends no further than payday,
Their contemplation ends before its heyday...,
Why study the past, the future is mayday,
Their present a task, each yeah a nay day!

Chapter 132

The Tremors of Tribulation

I ENVISION the sanctity of life,
Enshrined above mortal right...,
Think ahead, prevent, unwanted conception,
"Man" is not the origin of life!

I envision a republic with racial unity,
The issue is not race; it is Christ and antichrist...,
Life begets life, and death begets destruction,
He that is not with me is against me!

I envision a nation that won't compromise its principles,
With godless dictators or self appointed presidents...,
The shaking of hands between Gog and its allies,
Is about to shake more than you can imagine!

Since Oppenheimer's nuclear insights,
All hopes of the tranquil life are dashed...,
From explosions on transatlantic flights,
To Texas where our atoms are smashed!

The whore of Babylon is still alive and bleeding,
The life of the innocent both far and wide...,
Oh queen of Hollywood, thou city of sin,
Great harlot of Babylon now depicted in film!

America the free was the "Promised Land,"
The one we have bequeathed to sinister hands...,
Drug pushers, pornographers, black politic leeches,
Have sown the seed of tribulations flower!

Baltic States give way, unrest in China,
Communism decays, as Bush speaks louder...,
Proclaims, peace, peace, from the Malta summit,
Forgetting the past won't exempt you from it!

THE LAST PROPHET

The time of tribulation will follow,
The atomic holocaust on Earth...,
The souls that remain, will be as fodder,
When ravaging hordes come forth!

Some people will flee, and run to the mountains,
Others will conform to the beast...,
As they bend their knee, they betray their savior,
And seal their destinies!

CHAPTER 133

THE ASCENT TO THE SUMMIT

AT this very moment, the ascension of the "True Believers," whose names are written in the "Book of Life," is taking place. It is a process that has been going on for many cycles and incarnations. It has been a gradual advancement upward over time, to the extent that most people are totally unaware of its occurring. Even as there are those who do sense it and in a very real way, are cooperating with it.

The act of ascending is the process of proceeding from a lower level to a higher one. It is a matter of spiritual attainment and mastery, of one's knowledge accompanied by the correct use of that knowledge.

Every member of the human family has been in the act of ascendancy since their first human birth on earth. Some of them faster with more intent and some of them slower with less involvement, but all without fail.

However, there comes a time in the life of the soul, where one consciously takes oneself in hand, and enters on the spiritual path. It becomes imperative that a "Code of Life" and manner of living be initiated if true success is sought. The instruction set forth in the *Holy Bible* is man's "Code of Life," which is why it is called the "Book of Life."

For those on the spiritual path, there are some tried and tested techniques that the climber must use in order to get to the summit, and they should not be overlooked. The way leading up is fraught with dangers unseen, and obstacles unnoticed, until it is too late. The act of climbing becomes a matter of balance, continual balance and adjustment, if there is to be true gain.

The prerequisite to maintaining balance is unwavering obedience to "Divine Law," "Cosmic Law," "Natural Laws," and the "Social Laws." Divine laws are God's immutable laws and commandments. Cosmic laws are the universal laws of creation, both manifest and unmanifest. The natural laws govern the physical world. Social laws govern the commonwealth which are for the benefit of all.

The sum total of the laws that must be observed and obeyed in order for the aspirant to ascend the mountain of God include and exceed the "Laws of Moses," which are God's commandments. For instance, there is a "Cosmic Law of Non-Interference" in the lives of others, unless it is specifically requested. This law must also be respected, and adhered to, even though it is not one of the Ten Commandments, or a social convention.

By living in accordance with the sum of these laws and principles, we are able to safely move upward to higher ground, while maintaining balance. Through the continual act of obedience we are able to achieve stability in our daily lives, which is to stand on firm ground instead of shifting sand.

Adherences to the "Laws" are the principles required that will supply us with the skills necessary for the ascent. Until we understand the principles required for correct living, we will not be able to master the skills necessary for the ascent, and each climb will be a futile one. For every time we step outside of the law, we must inevitably and consistently suffer the recoil. The higher the climb, the further the fall, the harder the landing! Thus, as we move up higher to the summit of God attainment, the more crucial it becomes to maintain balance, and obedience, for each fall becomes exceedingly severe, and each recovery that much harder.

We can save ourselves a lot of time, energy, and much distress by scaling correctly. There will be failure, but it can be reduced, for balance cannot be sustained without continual obedience to God's manifold laws.

Take heed, dear friends, I know whereof I speak, and have nothing to gain by stressing such things, lest to remove some obstacles from your path!

Chapter 134

The Rescue of the Remnant

THE rescue of the remnant will be a dynamic and sudden event, prior to the final conflagration known as the "Battle of Armageddon."

It involves the rescuing and removal of those souls whose names are found written in the "Book of Life," from the planetary body, as foretold in the Bible, so that they will be preserved. They are the harvest of the first earth. They are the "Good Seed." They are God's "True Human" children who will populate the "New Jerusalem."

The names recorded therein, were known from the foundation of the world because the end was known from the beginning....

There is a time known to no man,
But as surely as the sun sets,
The hands of the clock will approach that hour,
The minute hand will turn in trepidation and awe,

To that fateful spot when all the gears,
Of the "Creator's Clock" line up,
The horn of Gabriel and Michael will sound,
It will be zero hour....

Jesus and his Legions will part the heavens...,
The dead in Christ will rise...,
And then the living...,
The "Great and Dreadful Day of the Lord" will begin!

Chapter 135

The Wake of Destruction

DESERT storms thru Kuwait, as Clinton debates,
With Barak and Arafat, no peace to create,
An election is fraud, as Gore is cheated,
A president by ruling, as Bush is seated!

Nine eleven reveals, New York's fate is sealed,
Down come the twin towers, the pentagon reels,
World war three begins, an enemy concealed,
The safety of America, Bin Laden steals!

Bombs rip through Afghanistan, daisy cutters used,
No enemy is found, but the war ensues,
Baghdad is blasted, its citizens strewn,
Hussein is captured, his foxhole room!

Great Britain is ambushed, Al Qaeda presumed,
As terror escalates, Bush visits the throne,
Vows to defeat terror, and around it goes,
Where it will stop, nobody knows!

CHAPTER 136

The Mountain of God

IN the beginning, there was a great and high mountain, where all things existed, yet slept in potential. All of creation was contained in that mountain, which is the seed of Creation. That mountain is God.

When God awoke, everything that slept sprung into existence, as in the blinking of an eye. In that instant, all things that were made were made whole, in that quantum moment in the heavens.

Man, his sojourns, the scriptures of his "Book of Life," and the Cosmos of creation were made whole. God saw the story of the history of man in a flash, therefore the end was known from the beginning....

God, in his mercy, had foreseen man's need for redemption in the day of reckoning, and so he provided a sacrifice, and gave his "Son" for the many. The only requirement is that we believe in him, and on him who sent him, to receive salvation.

The "End of Days" foretells the end of the story of the history of man. The "Day of Judgment" foretells the final consequences of man and his works. The "Day of Destruction" is at hand. Now is the appointed time for salvation....

There is an ark of safety, but there is only one escape route. There is a covenant between God and man that allows for salvation, but there is only one path and one portal. That path is up the mountain of God. That portal is through his Christ, his "Only Begotten Son," the doorway to "Eternal Life" is through the main gate!

It is the only safe haven in a crumbling world. It is the only place of refuge in a stormy sea. It is the only true rest in a world of unrest!

Chapter 137

The Sealed Book

AT the appointed times, God imparted man's "Book of Life" in portions, to the hearts and minds of the saints, and the prophets, until all portions of the book were complete. Later, the portions were compiled and canonized, and became the scriptures of today.

The *"Holy Bible"* is man's "Book of Life," which is also his "Code of Life!" God then issued a warning to all who would follow, that if anyone were to "add or take away" from the book, they would suffer the dire consequences within it. Any addition, or subtraction from the book would be tantamount to meddling with God's divine plan for the Human Race, thus it would corrupt the original "Word of God," or code, and that would interfere with man's system of beliefs, which would be detrimental to man's understanding and progress.

The Bible is man's "Code of Life" because it provides the system of rules necessary for man's correct spiritual growth, and it sets down man's system of laws to aid him in that quest, thus, the book provides a set of instructions for the human family....

John the Revelator, who wrote the divinely inspired "Book of Revelation," was carried away in the spirit, whereupon he saw the "End of Days." He witnessed the opening of the "Sealed Book," that none, save "One" could open. There were "Seven Seals" on the book, and as each of the "Seven Seals" were opened, he witnessed each of the "Seven Angels" in turn, come forth to pour out its contents. He then heard the voice of God, the "Almighty" command that the book be sealed until the time of the end.

Chapter 138

The Unsealed Book

MAN'S "Book of Life" was also imparted to the saints and prophets of old in the "original language" of the author. The original author is God. The original language is Hebrew. But within that Hebrew, is another two elements or layers of instruction that would at the appointed time be discovered and deciphered for the fulfillment of God's Will, and for the benefit of mankind.

The first element is the "encoded language" within the Bible that would be decoded at the time of the end, when the programmed language could be read, or extracted by the technology of today, the computer.

The second element is the "key" within the encoded language of the Bible that would, at the appointed time, be recognized and utilized by "the One who made the key" for the fulfillment of God's Will at the time of the end.

Thus, the "encoded language" of the Bible is one aspect. The "key" is the second aspect. The "encoded language" would be read, or extracted by "the one who discovers the code" at the time of the end. The "key" would be utilized by "the one who made the key" at the time of the end.

Thus, the "encoded language" of the Bible has been decoded, revealing not only its layer of instruction, but revealing the knowledge of the "key" to "the One who made the key," confirming absolutely that we are living in the time of the end.

The hidden code of the Bible that has been sought by sages, and scientists alike including Isaac Newton, was discovered by an Israeli mathematician named Eliyahu Rips, as told in Michael Drosnin's book, *"The Bible Code."* The Bible code does exist, but as Drosnin and Rips explain, they do not have all the pieces to the puzzle!

The reason for this being, the first element which is the "encoded language" within the Bible, was designed so that the second element, the "key" could be recognized and utilized by "the One who made the key" at the time of the end, in order to open the *"Holy Book"* or *"The Little Book"* and reveal its "Revelation."

Thus, the "key" would be utilized by "the one who made the key," and who shall be able to open that book, and loose the seals thereof? One thing is for certain, it shall be "the One who is worthy, and able, and authorized to do so!"

Michael Drosnin and Dr. Rips have uncovered many truths within the "encoded language" of the Bible, they have brought to light the probable future of the "End of Days," and have done well to issue the appropriate warnings to the appropriate players on the worldly stage.

In his globe-trotting efforts to avert a global catastrophe, Michael Drosnin's zeal has accomplished much more than he gives himself credit for, and may ultimately have altered the tide of affairs, and destruction that has been foretold.

I am equally grateful to the humble mathematician, Eliyahu Rips who discovered the actual "encoded language" in the Bible. Thus, he shall be known as "Eliyahu Rips, he who discovered the hidden language of the Bible in the End of Days." He has also done a superb job of unmasking and illuminating the true meaning of the "original language" of the scriptures, the sacred Hebrew.

But Michael Drosnin never definitively closes the book on the subject. He still seeks the elusive "key" that will "unlock" the total message, and bring the matter to a close....

In his second book, the "*Bible Code II, The Countdown*," Drosnin continues to seek, and sets out to find the "code key" buried in Lisan. He postulates the following in the last paragraph of his Coda, "in any event, it seems that the object we need, both to survive, and to gain the final insight, is the "code key" buried in Lisan."

In summary, he concludes, that a "key" buried somewhere in the "Lisan Valley" must be uncovered in order to reveal the complete and final message pertaining to the scriptures of the "*Holy Bible*."

His final proposal is that the "key" is buried in the "Lisan Valley" of Jordan. Of this he is exactly right, but what Michael Drosnin doesn't know, and couldn't know, is that the "Lisan Valley" is an allegory to a prophet, a "code" if you would, that could only be recognized by "the One who holds the key."

Thus, there are two "Lisan Valleys." One is the actual "Lisan Valley" where the salt sea used to be. The other "Lisan Valley," is a prophet, a prophet who lives in a valley, and within that prophet, the "key" to the mysteries of the "Bible Code" is buried.

Thus, "Lisan Valley" deciphered becomes "Lawson Valley," which becomes the "Valley of Lawson," which becomes "Valley Lawson," or "Dale Lawson," the "Last Prophet."

In this light, and seeing that the "*Holy Bible*" is the "Word of God," it would now indicate the last person, the last prophet to be certain, through whom God speaks to the multitudes, after which there is to be no other.

The sealed message of the "*Holy Bible*" will be unsealed by "the one who holds the key," and "the One who holds the key" would be well versed in the tone of the "original language," of the scriptures, and thus, would be able to expound the mysteries of that language for the benefit of all.

But language is more than the verbal communication of words of any one tongue or dialect. Language must be able to convey and express the true essence and intent of what is being communicated. One must be able to interpret the spirit of the law, as well as the letter of the law, and to be well versed in the "original language" of the author, means to be able to communicate in the same manner as the scriptures themselves.

One would have to speak in the same tone, and voice, and intent of the author. He would have to know how to exhort one to take righteous action, as did the Hebrew prophets of old. He would have to use biblical metaphor and symbol. He would know how to inspire, to incite, to put fear or wisdom in the hearts of its readers, for calamities sake. Above all, he would have to have been given the authority to impart the true meaning, spirit, and message of the writing, of which, there can only be one!

Thus, the discovery of the Bible Code's purpose has been served. This is to announce the arrival of "The Last Prophet" in the "End of Days," and to issue the Creator's final proclamation to the human population!

This language is the "Key!"

This key is the "Word!"

This word opens the "Book!"

This book hereby unseals the "Book of Revelation." It opens the "Seven Seals" thereof, so that the Creator's Will and its contents may be fulfilled, even unto its completion. It ushers in the "Lord's Day," and simultaneously sets the stage for the divine ending, the exodus of the remnant from the planetary body, those souls that have been redeemed from the foundation of the earth. The "Rapture" of the saints!

Therefore, "The Last Prophet" manuscript is the "Seal of the Prophets." It is the final and authoritative "Word of God" to the nations, through his prisoner and prophet.

Chapter 139

The Inner Vision

ALL around me I see disease, degeneration, and death,
And couldn't find more decay if I tried,
But don't be too quick, and label me pessimist...,
Truth is truth, what fails to live dies!

I have always sought to redeem mankind,
And yes, myself along with it,
So I address myself to the common man...,
Redemption begins with the individual!

I too, once stuck to the premise,
That the world was progressively getting better,
Though the law of motion demonstrates...,
When momentum slows, progression folds!

Is it possible to maintain the illusion of movement?
Progress is apparent, midst stagnation and inertia,
Stagnation breeds disease, inertia death...,
The prophet said, "Without vision, the people perish!"

Chapter 140

THE LAW DIVINE

THE world is deluded and knows it not,
The norm of the day, self indulgence,
The vision of men, despicably wrought...,
Who shall regain divine direction?

The sovereignty is confuted by standards lost,
Drowning in a sea of astral substance,
The souls of men, woefully drought...,
Who shall survive such spiritual famine?

Drifting in a sea without rudder or compass,
A ship of fools, I deign to agree,
No wind in the sails, or sails in the wind...,
What good will paths or charts do you?

To know where you are going, you must know where you have been,
To know that you are lost is respectable indeed,
By following God's law, you regain the direction...,
Then right living is the sail, in destinies wind!

Chapter 141

The Power Supreme

DO you strive for peace daily?
Would you experience true brotherhood,
In your comings and goings?
Would you be exalted in laughter?
Love is the shortest distance between two points!

Would you soften blunt interactions?
Do you seek the good in every man?
Would you give a moment to one in need,
To gain an hour of heavenly deed?
Love is the path of least resistance!

Can you accept the blame for another's failure?
Could you fail to praise a worldly idol?
Would you affirm the Christ midst hostility,
Forgive the atheist his temporary doubt?
Love is greater than pity!

Would you wander the earth undaunted?
Could you cast off the illusion of security?
Would you embark on new seas with trust and welcome,
Face turmoil with poise, chance with understanding?
Perfect love casts out all fear!

Chapter 142

The Blessing of Israel

BROTHERS unite, love's power supreme,
The universe is light!
Fire ignite the nucleus of being,
Consume the shadow of night!

Sisters rejoice, oh heavenly vessels,
Thy wombs are rooms of light!
Violet fire prepare the alchemical leaven,
Make way for souls of Christ!

Children delight, love's playful dream,
The future is bright!
Spirit excite and raise the vibration,
Of all creation forthright!

Chapter 143

The True Human

THE being of man is the expression of love....
The body of man, the vessel of love....
The soul of man is the potential of love....
The spirit of man, the excellence of love!

The nature of man is the quest of love....
The want of man, the feeling of love....
The need of man is the experience of love....
The goal of man, the perfection of love!

The business of man is the promotion of love....
The work of man, the execution of love....
The recreation of man is the dance of love....
The purpose of man, the expanse of love!

The mind of man is the map of love....
The heart of man, the treasure of love....
The realization of man is the discovery of love....
The illumination of man, the proof of love!

Chapter 144

The Crown of Life

NOT thinking anything, doing less,
The sunshine reigns upon us.
Sitting..., walking..., looking..., feeling...,
Sun-drops of love light around us!

Not doing anything, being more,
The world is alone perfect.
Evolving..., turning..., still..., revolving...,
Planets of pearls none imperfect!

Not being anyone, self dissolves,
Selfless in God's self whole.
Being..., knowing..., ebbing..., flowing...,
Godhood winning is the goal!

CODA

"AND I saw a new heaven and a new earth:
For the first heaven and the first earth were passed away;
And there was no more sea."

"And he that sat upon the throne said, Behold, I make all things new.
And he said unto me, Write: for these words are true and faithful."

"And he said unto me, It is done.
I am Alpha and Omega, the beginning and the end.
I will give unto him that is athirst of the fountain of the water of life freely."

"He that overcometh shall inherit all things;
And I will be his God, and he shall be my son."

"And he carried me away in the spirit to a great and high mountain,
And shewed me that great city, the holy Jerusalem,
Descending out of heaven from God."

"And had a wall great and high, *and* had twelve gates,
And at the gates twelve angels, and names written thereon,
Which are *the names* of the twelve tribes of the children of Israel."

- Revelation 21: 1, 5, 6, 7, 10, 12

AFTERTHOUGHT

IT troubles me that modern man refers to our "Creator" so sparingly in their busy lives, for fear of what others may think, and then only in innocuous situations, where they do not have to take sides. As was said previously, the "Son of Man" will not recognize any who do recognize him, when he comes into his kingdom. A word to the wise should be sufficient, we shall see....

The ancients and wise men of old had only to think of our "Divine Source" and would have to recompose themselves. That is why they referred to him as "the One of whom naught shall be said." That kind of humility is the need of the hour, it is the prescription for today, and the prognosis for tomorrow!

All the "Son of Man" asked of men, was that they build a bridge to him through love, and in love, knocks upon his door, seeking to know him. By virtue of knowing him, they would be converted to "Everlasting Life."

This is the "Gift of God" and the encoded message in the "*Holy Bible*" if ever there was one. This is it in a nutshell. If you are seeking something more, you have missed the point!

"And this is his commandment,
That we should believe on the name of his Son Jesus Christ,
And love one another, as he gave us commandment."

- 1 John 3: 23

"And this is the record,
That God hath given to us eternal life,
And this life is in his Son."

- 1 John 5: 11

The real sorrow of the ages will surely be that the multitudes, the proud and the busy, the rich and the vain, the lazy and the uncouth, have never sought him at all. The *"True Tragedy"* will be those who never took the time to build a bridge to their own salvation. Those who neither wanted him in their lives, nor helped him shoulder the burden of the cross when the wood was green, how much less so now that the wood is dry.

DALE LAWSON																					ONE MALE

THE END

Definitions and Terms

"Ancient"

Of times long past, belonging to the early history of the world,
Having existed a long time, very old, a person who lived in ancient times!

"Herald"

A person who proclaims or announces significant news,
A person that comes before what follows, forerunner, harbinger,
To introduce, announce, foretell, and usher in!

"Ancient Herald"

A person, or messenger, of times long past,
Who comes to announce significant news!
A prophet who comes to announce what follows,
One who comes to usher in!

"Ancient of Days"

God or a heavenly judge!

Definitions and Terms

"Last"

Late, being or coming after all others in place or time,
The only remaining, utmost, conclusive, authoritative!

"Prophet"

Interpreter of a god's will,
An inspired preacher, a person who speaks for God, or a god,
Or as though under divine guidance, a religious teacher or leader,
A person who predicts future events!

"Last Prophet"

The term "Last Prophet" is used in religious contexts to refer to
The "Last Person" through whom God speaks to the people,
After which there is to be no other!

"Seal of the Prophets"

The term "Seal of the Prophets" is used in religious contexts to refer to
The final and authoritative prophet in a succession of prophets,
That is "The Last Prophet!"

REFERENCE SCRIPTURE

ALL scripture quoted in "THE LAST PROPHET" manuscript has been taken from the "AUTHORIZED KING JAMES VERSION" of:

THE
HOLY BIBLE

CONTAINING THE

OLD AND NEW TESTAMENTS

TRANSLATED OUT OF THE ORIGINAL TONGUES:
AND WITH THE FORMER TRANSLATIONS
DILIGENTLY COMPARED AND REVISED,
BY HIS MAJESTY'S SPECIAL COMMAND

CONCORDANCE

PUBLISHED BY
THE SYNDICS OF THE CAMBRIDGE UNIVERSITY PRESS
Bentley House, 200 Euston Road, London, N.W.1

PRINTED IN GREAT BRITAIN
AT THE UNIVERSITY PRINTING HOUSE, CAMBRIDGE

Chapter 1

The Human Race

"AND if it seem evil unto you to serve the Lord, choose you this day whom ye will serve; whether the gods which your fathers served that *were* on the other side of the flood, or the gods of the Amorites, in whose land ye dwell: but as for me and my house, we will serve the Lord."

- Joshua 24: 15

"Behold, a sower went forth to sow."

- Matthew 13: 3

"But one in a certain place testified, saying, What is man, that thou art mindful of him? or the son of man, that thou visitest him?"

- Hebrews 2: 6

"For verily he took not on *him the nature of* angels; but he took on *him* the seed of Abraham."

- Hebrews 2: 16

"For what *is* your life? It is even a vapour, that appeareth for a little time, and then vanisheth away."

- James 4: 14

Chapter 2

The Veiled Mind

"AND the light shineth in darkness; and the darkness comprehended it not."

- John 1: 5

"This I say therefore, and testify in the Lord, that ye henceforth walk not as other Gentiles walk, in the vanity of their mind."

- Ephesians 4: 17

"Which *hope* we have as an anchor of the soul, both sure and steadfast, and which entereth into that within the veil."

- Hebrews 6: 19

"Now faith is the substance of things hoped for, the evidence of things not seen."

- Hebrews 11: 1

"Dearly beloved, I beseech *you* as strangers and pilgrims, abstain from fleshly lusts, which war against the soul."

- 1 Peter 2: 11

Chapter 3

# The Clouded Mind

"MY confusion *is* continually before me, and the shame of my face hath covered me."

- Psalms 44: 15

"In thee, O Lord, do I put my trust: let me never be put to confusion."

- Psalms 71: 1

"O Lord, righteousness *belongeth* unto thee, but unto us confusion of faces, as at this day; to the men of Judah, and to the inhabitants of Jerusalem, and unto all Israel, *that are* near, and *that are* far off, through all the countries whither thou hast driven them, because of their trespass that they have trespassed against thee."

- Daniel 9: 7

"O Lord, to us *belongeth* confusion of face, to our kings, to our princes, and to our fathers, because we have sinned against thee."

- Daniel 9: 8

"For God is not *the author* of confusion, but of peace, as in all churches of the saints."

- 1 Corinthians 14: 33

"Having the understanding darkened, being alienated from the life of God through the ignorance that is in them, because of the blindness of their heart."

- Ephesians 4: 18

Chapter 4

The Dual Nature of Man

"CAST out the scorner, and contention shall go out; yea, strife and reproach shall cease."

- Proverbs 22: 10

"But that which beareth thorns and briers *is* rejected, and *is* nigh unto cursing; whose end *is* to be burned."

- Hebrews 6: 8

"A double minded man *is* unstable in all his ways."

- James 1: 8

"Grudge not one against another, brethren, lest ye be condemned: behold, the judge standeth before the door."

- James 5: 9

"Knowing this first, that there shall come in the last days scoffers, walking after their own lusts."

- 2 Peter 3: 3

"These are murmurers, complainers, walking after their own lusts; and their mouth speaketh great swelling words, having men's persons in admiration because of advantage."

- Jude 1: 16

CHAPTER 5

THE AFFLICTION

"MAN *that is* born of a woman *is* of few days, and full of trouble."

- Job 14: 1

"He hath put my brethren far from me, and mine acquaintances are verily estranged from me."

- Job 19: 13

"Look upon my affliction and my pain; and forgive all my sins."

- Psalms 25: 18

"And Jesus knew their thoughts, and said unto them, Every kingdom divided against itself is brought to desolation; and every city or house divided against itself shall not stand."

- Matthew 12: 25

"Be not thou therefore ashamed of the testimony of our Lord, nor of me his prisoner: but be thou partaker of the afflictions of the gospel according to the power of God."

- 2 Timothy 1: 8

"Is any among you afflicted? Let him pray...."

- James 5: 13

Chapter 6

The Illusory Dream

"FOR a dream cometh through the multitude of business; and a fool's voice *is known* by multitude of words."

- Ecclesiastes 5: 3

"And every one that heareth these sayings of mine, and doeth them not, shall be likened unto a foolish man, which built his house upon the sand."

- Matthew 7: 26

"And he cometh unto the disciples, and findeth them asleep, and saith unto Peter, What, could ye not watch with me one hour?"

- Matthew 26: 40

"Looking unto Jesus the author and finisher of *our* faith; who for the joy that was set before him endured the cross, despising the shame, and is set down at the right hand of the throne of God."

- Hebrews 12: 2

"We have also a more sure word of prophecy: where unto ye do well that ye take heed, as unto a light that shineth in a dark place, until the day dawn, and the day star arise in your hearts."

- 2 Peter 1: 19

Chapter 7

The Prodigal Path

"I GO the way of all the earth: be thou strong therefore, and shew thyself a man."

- 1 Kings 2: 2

"This *is* not the way, neither *is* this the city: follow me, and I will bring you to the man whom ye seek...."

- 2 Kings 6: 19

"God hath delivered me to the ungodly, and turned me over into the hands of the wicked."

- Job 16: 11

"*It is* God that girdeth me with strength, and maketh my way perfect."

- Psalms 18: 32

"There is a way that seemeth right unto a man, but the end thereof *are* the ways of death."

- Proverbs 16: 25

"But seek ye first the kingdom of God, and his righteousness; and all these things shall be added unto you."

- Matthew 6: 33

Chapter 8

 The Lost Soul

"AND the Lord sent thee on a journey…"

- 1 Samuel 15: 18

"Then shall the trees of the wood sing out at the presence of the Lord, because he cometh to judge the earth."

- 1 Chronicles 16: 33

"For who *is* God save the Lord? or who *is* a rock save our God?"

- Psalms 18: 31

"For thou *art* my rock and my fortress; therefore for thy name's sake lead me, and guide me."

- Psalms 31: 3

"In all thy ways acknowledge him, and he shall direct thy paths."

- Proverbs 3: 6

"Rejoice with them that do rejoice, and weep with them that weep."

- Romans 12: 15

"Jesus Christ the same yesterday, and to day, and for ever."

- Hebrews 13: 8

CHAPTER 9

THE DIVINE CONVICTION

"BEFORE I was afflicted I went astray: but now have I kept thy word."

- Psalms 119: 67

"And an highway shall be there, and a way, and it shall be called The way of holiness; the unclean shall not pass over it; but it *shall be* for those: the wayfaring men, though fools, shall not err *therein*."

- Isaiah 35: 8

"I, even I, am he that blotteth out thy transgressions."

- Isaiah 43: 25

"For if the casting away of them *be* the reconciling of the world, what *shall* the receiving *of them be*, but life from the dead?"

- Romans 11: 15

"Herein is love, not that we loved God, but that he loved us, and sent his Son *to be* the propitiation for our sins."

- 1 John 4: 10

Chapter 10

The Laws of Life

"IN the way of righteousness *is* life; and *in* the pathway *thereof there is* no death."

- Proverbs 12: 28

"Think not that I am come to destroy the law, or the prophets: I am not come to destroy, but to fulfill."

- Matthew 5: 17

"For verily I say unto you, Till heaven and earth pass, one jot or one tittle shall in no wise pass from the law, till all be fulfilled."

- Matthew 5: 18

"And he said unto him, Why callest thou me good? *there is* none good but one, *that is*, God: but if thou wilt enter into life, keep the commandments."

- Matthew 19: 17

"Now the end of the commandment is charity out of a pure heart, and *of* a good conscience, and *of* faith unfeigned."

- Timothy 1: 5

"Honour all men. Love the brotherhood. Fear God. Honour the king."

- 1 Peter 2: 17

"And this is love, that we walk after his commandments…"

- 2 John 1: 6

Chapter 11

The Beat of Life

"O THAT there were such an heart in them, that they would fear me, and keep all my commandments always, that it might be well with them, and with their children for ever."

- Deuteronomy 5: 29

"Is thine heart right, as my heart *is* with thy heart...?"

- 2 Kings 10: 15

"With my whole heart have I sought thee: O let me not wander from thy commandments."

- Psalms 119: 10

"Keep thy heart with all diligence; for out of it *are* the issues of life."

- Proverbs 4: 23

"Who can say, I have made my heart clean, I am pure from my sin?"

- Proverbs 20: 9

"And they said one to another, Did not our heart burn within us, while he talked with us by the way, and while he opened to us the scriptures?"

- Luke 24: 32

Chapter 12

The Hum of Life

"BLESSED *is* the people that know the joyful sound: they shall walk, O Lord, in the light of thy countenance."

- Psalms 89: 15

"Let them praise his name in the dance: let them sing praises unto him with the timbrel and harp."

- Psalms 149: 3

"The flowers appear on the earth; the time of the singing *of birds* is come, and the voice of the turtle is heard in our land."

- The Song of Solomon 2: 12

"What is it then? I will pray with the spirit, and I will pray with the understanding also: I will sing with the spirit, and I will sing with the understanding also."

- 1 Corinthians 14: 15

"Speaking to yourselves in psalms and hymns and spiritual songs, singing and making melody in your heart to the Lord."

- Ephesians 5: 19

Chapter 13

The Mirror Image

"I WAS cast upon thee from the womb: thou *art* my God from my mother's belly."

- Psalms 22: 10

"For now we see through a glass, darkly; but then face to face: now I know in part; but then shall I know even as also I am known."

- 1 Corinthians 13: 12

"But we all, with open face beholding as in a glass the glory of the Lord, are changed into the same image from glory to glory, *even* as by the Spirit of the Lord."

- 2 Corinthians 3: 18

"Who is the image of the invisible God, the firstborn of every creature."

- Colossians 1: 15

"For if any be a hearer of the word, and not a doer, he is like unto a man beholding his natural face in a glass."

- James 1: 23

"For this they willingly are ignorant of, that by the word of God the heavens were of old, and the earth standing out of the water and in the water."

- 2 Peter 3: 5

Chapter 14

The Base of Creation

"IN the beginning God created the heaven and the earth."

- Genesis 1: 1

"And in very deed for this *cause* have I raised thee up, for to shew *in* thee my power; and that my name may be declared throughout all the earth."

- Exodus 9: 16

"The heavens declare the glory of God; and the firmament sheweth his handywork."

- Psalms 19: 1

"O Lord, how manifold are thy works! In wisdom hast thou made them all: the earth is full of thy riches."

- Psalms 104: 24

"Praise ye the Lord. Praise God in his sanctuary: praise him in the firmament of his power."

- Psalms 150: 1

"That they may see, and know, and consider, and understand together, that the hand of the Lord hath done this, and the Holy One of Israel hath created it."

- Isaiah 41: 20

Chapter 15

The Creator's Clock

"AND he changeth the times and the seasons: he removeth kings, and setteth up kings..."

- Daniel 2: 21

"I beheld till the thrones were cast down, and the Ancient of days did sit, whose garment *was* white as snow, and the hair of his head like the pure wool: his throne *was like* the fiery flame, *and* his wheels *as* burning fire."

- Daniel 7: 9

"A fiery stream issued and came forth from before him: thousand thousands ministered unto him, and ten thousand times ten thousand stood before him: the judgment was set, and the books were opened."

- Daniel 7: 10

"And he said unto them, It is not for you to know the times or the seasons, which the Father hath put in his own power."

- Acts 1: 7

"And hath made of one blood all nations of men for to dwell on all the face of the earth, and hath determined the times before appointed, and the bounds of their habitation."

- Acts 17: 26

"But beloved, be not ignorant of this one thing, that one day *is* with the Lord as a thousand years, and a thousand years as one day."

- 2 Peter 3: 8

Chapter 16

The Vine of Life

"AND now, O inhabitants of Jerusalem, and men of Judah, judge, I pray you, betwixt me and my vineyard."

- Isaiah 5: 3

"What could have been done more to my vineyard, that I have not done in it? wherefore, when I looked that it should bring forth grapes, brought it forth wild grapes?"

- Isaiah 5: 4

"And now go to; I will tell you what I will do to my vineyard: I will take away the hedge thereof, and it shall be eaten up; *and* break down the wall thereof, and it shall be trodden down."

- Isaiah 5: 5

"And I will lay it waste: it shall not be pruned, nor digged; but there shall come up briers and thorns: I will also command the clouds that they rain no rain upon it."

- Isaiah 5: 6

"For the vineyard of the Lord of hosts *is* the house of Israel, and the men of Judah his pleasant plant."

- Isaiah 5: 7

"For if the firstfruit *be* holy, the lump *is* also *holy*: and if the root *be* holy, so *are* the branches."

- Romans 11: 16

Chapter 17

The Main Gate

"ASK, and it shall be given you; seek, and ye shall find; knock, and it shall be opened unto you."

- Matthew 7: 7

"Jesus saith unto him, I am the way, the truth, and the life: no man cometh unto the Father, but by me."

- John 14: 6

"For *there is* one God, and one mediator between God and men, the man Christ Jesus."

- Timothy 2: 5

"So we see that they could not enter in because of unbelief."

- Hebrews 3: 19

"Blessed *are* they that do his commandments, that they may have right to the tree of life, and may enter in through the gates into the city."

- Revelation 22: 14

Chapter 18

The Wedding Day

"AND he saith unto him, Friend, how camest thou in hither not having a wedding garment? And he was speechless."

- Matthew 22: 12

"And ye yourselves like unto men that wait for their lord, when he will return from the wedding; that when he cometh and knocketh, they may open unto him immediately."

- Luke 12: 36

"Blessed *are* those servants, whom the lord when he cometh shall find watching: verily I say unto you, that he shall gird himself, and make them to sit down to meat, and will come forth and serve them."

- Luke 12: 37

"Be ye therefore ready also: for the Son of man cometh at an hour when ye think not."

- Luke 12: 40

"And he saith unto me, Write, Blessed *are* they which are called unto the marriage supper of the Lamb."

- Revelation 19: 9

Chapter 19

The Day of Rapture

"THE Lord also shall roar out of Zion, and utter his voice from Jerusalem; and the heavens and the earth shall shake: but the Lord *will be* the hope of his people, and the strength of the children of Israel."

- Joel 3: 16

"Let your loins be girded about, and *your* lights burning."

- Luke 12: 35

"Looking for that blessed hope, and the glorious appearing of the great God and our saviour Jesus Christ."

- Titus 2: 13

"But the end of all things is at hand: be ye therefore sober, and watch unto prayer."

- 1 Peter 4: 7

"Let us be glad and rejoice, and give honour to him: for the marriage of the Lamb is come, and his wife hath made herself ready."

- Revelation 19: 7

"Behold, I come quickly: blessed *is* he that keepeth the sayings of the prophecy of this book."

- Revelation 22: 7

CHAPTER 20

THE GIFT OF LIFE

"FOR unto us a child is born, unto us a son is given: and the government shall be upon his shoulder: and his name shall be called Wonderful, Counsellor, The mighty God, The everlasting Father, The Prince of Peace."

- Isaiah 9: 6

"But when the fulness of the time was come, God sent forth his Son, made of a woman, made under the law."

- Galatians 4: 4

"To redeem them that were under the law..."

- Galatians 4: 5

"For such an high priest became us, *who is* holy, harmless, undefiled, separate from sinners, and made higher than the heavens."

- Hebrews 7: 26

"I am Alpha and Omega, the beginning and the ending, saith the Lord, which is and which was, and which is to come, the Almighty."

- Revelation 1: 8

"And she brought forth a man child, who was to rule all nations with a rod of iron: and her child was caught up unto God, and *to* his throne."

- Revelation 12: 5

Chapter 21

 The Gift of Innocence

"THOU sendest forth thy spirit, they are created: and thou renewest the face of the earth."

- Psalms 104: 30

"Lo, children *are* an heritage of the Lord: *and* the fruit of the womb *is his* reward."

- Psalms 127: 3

"Children's children *are* the crown of old men; and the glory of children *are* their fathers."

- Proverbs 17: 6

"Train up a child in the way he should go: and when he is old, he will not depart from it."

- Proverbs 22: 6

"And the streets of the city shall be full of boys and girls playing in the streets thereof."

- Zechariah 8: 5

Chapter 22

The Day of Initiation

"FOR thou wilt light my candle: the Lord my God will enlighten my darkness."

- Psalms 18: 28

"The statutes of the Lord *are* right, rejoicing the heart: the commandment of the Lord *is* pure, enlightening the eyes."

- Psalms 19: 8

"Now it came to pass in the thirtieth year, in the fourth *month*, in the fifth *day* of the month, as I *was* among the captives by the river of Chebar, *that* the heavens were opened, and I saw visions of God."

- Ezekiel 1: 1

"And he went forth again by the sea side; and all the multitude resorted unto him, and he taught them."

- Mark 2: 13

"The eyes of your understanding being enlightened; that ye may know what is the hope of his calling, and what the riches of the glory of his inheritance in the saints."

- Ephesians 1: 18

Chapter 23

The Baptism of Fire

"MY soul *is* among lions: *and* I lie *even among* them that are set on fire, *even* the sons of men, whose teeth *are* spears and arrows, and their tongue a sharp sword."

- Psalms 57: 4

"Wherefore glorify ye the Lord in the fires, even the name of the Lord God of Israel in the isles of the sea."

- Isaiah 24: 15

"Wherefore thus saith the Lord God of hosts, Because ye speak this word, behold, I will make my words in thy mouth fire, and this people wood, and it shall devour them."

- Jeremiah 5: 14

"But who may abide the day of his coming? and who shall stand when he appeareth? for he *is* like a refiner's fire, and like fuller's soap."

- Malachi 3: 2

"I indeed baptize you with water unto repentance: but he that cometh after me is mightier than I, whose shoes I am not worthy to bear: he shall baptize you with the Holy Ghost, and *with* fire."

- Matthew 3: 11

Chapter 24

The Holy Communion

"BUT the Lord *is* in his holy temple: let all the earth keep silence before him."

- Habakkuk 2: 20

"Verily I say unto you, except ye be converted, and become as little children, ye shall not enter into the kingdom of heaven."

- Matthew 18: 3

"And the angel answered and said unto her, The Holy Ghost shall come upon thee, and the power of the Highest shall over shadow thee: therefore also that holy thing which shall be born of thee shall be called the Son of God."

- Luke 1: 35

"For both he that sanctifieth and they who are sanctified *are* all of one..."

- Hebrews 2: 11

"This is he that came by water and blood, *even* Jesus Christ; not by water only, but by water and blood. And it is the Spirit that beareth witness, because the Spirit is truth."

- 1 John 5: 6

Chapter 25

The Hallowed Child

"SAYING, Touch not mine anointed, and do my prophets no harm."

- 1 Chronicles 16: 22

"Shall mortal man be more just than God? shall a man be more pure than his maker?"

- Job 4: 17

"And one cried unto another, and said, Holy, holy, holy, *is* the Lord of hosts: the whole earth *is* full of his glory."

- Isaiah 6: 3

"By him therefore let us offer the sacrifice of praise to God continually, that is, the fruit of *our lips* giving thanks to his name."

- Hebrews 13: 15

"For he received from God the Father honour and glory, when there came such a voice to him from the excellent glory, This is my beloved Son, in whom I am well pleased."

- 2 Peter 1: 17

Chapter 26

The Spiritual Mind

"WHO coverest *thyself* with light as *with* a garment: who stretchest out the heavens like a curtain."

- Psalms 104: 2

"The lips of the righteous feed many: but fools die for want of wisdom."

- Proverbs 10: 21

"Godly men are growing a tree that bears life-giving fruit."

- Proverbs 11: 30

"For as the rain cometh down, and the snow from heaven, and returneth not thither, but watereth the earth, and maketh it bring forth and bud, that it may give seed to the sower, and bread to the eater."

- Isaiah 55: 10

"Every plant, which my heavenly Father hath not planted, shall be rooted up."

- Matthew 15: 13

"Distributing to the necessity of saints; given to hospitality."

- Romans 12: 13

Chapter 27

The Carnal Mind

"THEREFORE shall a man leave his father and his mother, and shall cleave unto his wife: and they shall be one flesh."

- Genesis 2: 24

"For we know that the law is spiritual: but I am carnal, sold under sin."

- Romans 7: 14

"For I delight in the law of God after the inward man."

- Romans 7: 22

"But I see another law in my members, warring against the law of my mind, and bringing me into captivity to the law of sin which is in my members."

- Romans 7: 23

"For to be carnally minded *is* death; but to be spiritually minded *is* life and peace."

- Romans 8: 6

"For if ye live after the flesh, ye shall die: but if ye through the Spirit do mortify the deeds of the body, ye shall live."

- Romans 8: 13

"These be they who separate themselves, sensual, having not the spirit."

- Jude 1: 19

Chapter 28

The Fall from Grace

"FOR sin, taking occasion by the commandment, deceived me, and by it slew *me*."

- Romans 7: 11

"For the good that I would I do not: but the evil which I would not, that I do."

- Romans 7: 19

"I find then a law, that, when I would do good, evil is present with me."

- Romans 7: 21

"O wretched man that I am! who shall deliver me from the body of this death?"

- Romans 7: 24

"For in that he himself hath suffered being tempted, he is able to succour them that are tempted."

- Hebrews 2: 18

"Looking diligently lest any man fail of the grace of God; lest any root of bitterness springing up trouble *you*, and thereby many be defiled."

- Hebrews 12: 15

Chapter 29

"WATCH and pray, that ye enter not into temptation: the spirit indeed *is* willing, but the flesh *is* weak."

- Matthew 26: 41

"Now the works of the flesh are manifest, which are these; Adultery, fornication, uncleanness, lasciviousness, idolatry, witchcraft, hatred, variance, emulations, wrath, strife, seditions, heresies, envyings, murders, drunkenness, revellings, and such like: of the which I tell you before, as I have also told *you* in time past, that they which do such things shall not inherit the kingdom of God."

- Galatians 5: 19, 20, 21

"For he that wavereth is like a wave of the sea driven with the wind and tossed."

- James 1: 6

"Blessed *is* the man that endureth temptation: for when he is tried, he shall receive the crown of life, which the Lord hath promised to them that love him."

- James 1: 12

"The Lord knoweth how to deliver the godly out of temptation, and to reserve the unjust unto the day of judgment to be punished."

- 2 Peter 2: 9

Chapter 30

The Crossroads of Life

"AS *for* God, his way *is* perfect: the word of the Lord is tried: he *is* a buckler to all those that trust in him."

- Psalms 18: 30

"Wherewithal shall a young man cleanse his way? by taking heed *thereto* according to thy word."

- Psalms 119: 9

"Ponder the path of thy feet, and let all thy ways be established."

- Proverbs 4: 26

"A man's heart deviseth his way: but the Lord directeth his steps."

- Proverbs 16: 9

"Hear counsel, and receive instruction, that thou mayest be wise in thy latter end."

- Proverbs 19: 20

"Multitudes, multitudes in the valley of decision: for the day of the Lord *is* near in the valley of decision."

- Joel 3: 14

Chapter 31

The Coin of the Realm

"BUT the Lord said unto Samuel, Look not on his countenance, or on the height of his stature; because I have refused him: for *the Lord seeth* not as man seeth; for man looketh on the outward appearance, but the Lord looketh on the heart."

- 1 Samuel 16: 7

"The fining pot *is* for silver, and the furnace for gold: but the Lord trieth the hearts."

- Proverbs 17: 3

"And I will give unto thee the keys of the kingdom of heaven: and whatsoever thou shalt bind on earth shall be bound in heaven: and whatsoever thou shalt loose on earth shall be loosed in heaven."

- Matthew 16: 19

"For whom the Lord loveth he chasteneth, and scourgeth every son whom he receives."

- Hebrews 12: 6

"For our God *is* a consuming fire."

- Hebrews 12: 29

"His eyes *were* as a flame of fire, and on his head *were* many crowns; and he had a name written, that no man knew, but he himself."

- Revelation 19: 12

Chapter 32

The Rod of Obedience

"AND Samuel said, Hath the Lord *as great* delight in burnt offerings and sacrifices, as in obeying the voice of the Lord? Behold, to obey *is* better than sacrifice, *and* to hearken than the fat of rams."

- 1 Samuel 15: 22

"Then will I visit their transgression with the rod, and their iniquity with stripes."

- Psalms 89: 32

"He that keepeth the commandment keepeth his own soul; *but* he that despiseth his ways shall die."

- Proverbs 19: 16

"Chasten thy son while there is hope, and let not thy soul spare for his crying."

- Proverbs 19: 18

"Foolishness *is* bound in the heart of a child; *but* the rod of correction shall drive it far from him."

- Proverbs 22: 15

"What will ye? shall I come unto you with a rod, or in love, and *in* the spirit of meekness?"

- 1 Corinthians 4: 21

Chapter 33

The Key to Reparation

"LET the priests take *it* to them, every man of his acquaintance: and let them repair the breaches of the house, wheresoever any breach shall be found."

- 2 Kings 12: 5

"And it came to pass after this, *that* Joash was minded to repair the house of the Lord."

- 2 Chronicles 24: 4

"Behold, I cry out of wrong, but I am not heard: I cry aloud, but *there is* no judgment."

- Job 19: 7

"Ye have not gone up into the gaps, neither made up the hedge for the house of Israel to stand in the battle in the day of the Lord."

- Ezekiel 13: 5

"And I sought for a man among them, that should make up the hedge, and stand in the gap before me for the land, that I should not destroy it: but I found none."

- Ezekiel 22: 30

Chapter 34

The Realization of Truth

"THINE own mouth condemneth thee, and not I: yea, thine own lips testify against thee."

- Job 15: 6

"Lift up your heads, O ye gates; and be ye lift up, ye everlasting doors; and the King of glory shall come in."

- Psalms 24: 7

"Truth shall spring out of the earth; and righteousness shall look down from heaven."

- Psalms 85: 11

"For the Lord *is* our judge, the Lord *is* our lawgiver, the Lord *is* our king; he will save us."

- Isaiah 33: 22

"Then opened he their understanding, that they might understand the scriptures."

- Luke 24: 45

CHAPTER 35

THE KEY TO HARMONY

"AND the Lord God took the man, and put him into the garden of Eden to dress it and to keep it."

- Genesis 2: 15

"Man goeth forth unto his work and to his labour until the evening."

- Psalms 104: 23

"The fig tree putteth forth her green figs, and the vines *with* the tender grape give a *good* smell. Arise, my love, my fair one, and come away."

- The Song of Solomon 2: 13

"My beloved *is* mine, and I *am* his…"

- The Song of Solomon 2: 16

"Awake, O north wind; and come, thou south; blow upon my garden, *that* the spices thereof may flow out. Let my beloved come into his garden…"

- The Song of Solomon 3: 16

"For the Lord shall comfort Zion: he will comfort all her waste places; and he will make her wilderness like Eden, and her desert like the garden of the Lord; joy and gladness shall be found therein, thanksgiving, and the voice of melody."

- Isaiah 51: 3

Chapter 36

The Measure of a Man

"THINE, O Lord, *is* the greatness, and the power, and the glory, and the victory, and the majesty: for all *that is* in the heaven and in the earth *is thine*; thine *is* the kingdom, O Lord, and thou art exalted as head above all."

- 1 Chronicles 29: 11

"I will praise thee; for I am fearfully *and* wonderfully made: marvellous *are* thy works; and *that* my soul knoweth right well."

- Psalms 139: 14

"My substance was not hid from thee, when I was made in secret, *and* curiously wrought in the lowest parts of the earth."

- Psalms 139: 15

"Who hath measured the waters in the hollow of his hand, and meted out heaven with the span, and comprehended the dust of the earth in a measure, and weighed the mountains in scales, and the hills in a balance."

- Isaiah 40: 12

"Now he that planteth and he that watereth are one: and every man shall receive his own reward according to his own labour."

- 1 Corinthians 3: 8

"For we are labourers together with God: ye *are* God's husbandry, ye are God's building."

- 1 Corinthians 3: 9

Chapter 37

The Considerate

"LET the words of my mouth, and the meditation of my heart, be acceptable in thy sight, O Lord, my strength, and my redeemer."

- Psalms 19: 14

"Now therefore thus saith the Lord of Hosts; Consider your ways."

- Haggai 1: 5

"But love ye your enemies, and do good, and lend, hoping for nothing again; and your reward shall be great, and ye shall be the children of the Highest: for he is kind unto the unthankful and to the evil."

- Luke 6: 35

"Let brotherly love continue."

- Hebrews 13: 1

"And who *is* he that will harm you, if ye be followers of that which is good?"

- 1 Peter 3: 13

"For *it is* better, if the will of God be so, that ye suffer for well doing, than for evil doing."

- 1 Peter 3: 17

Chapter 38

The Divine Immunity

"A GOOD *man* obtaineth favour of the Lord: but a man of wicked devices will he condemn."

- Proverbs 12: 2

"The wicked are overthrown, and *are* not: but the house of the righteous shall stand."

- Proverbs 12: 7

"The evil bow before the good; and the wicked at the gates of the righteous."

- Proverbs 14: 19

"When a man's ways please the Lord, he maketh even his enemies to be at peace with him."

- Proverbs 16: 7

"But the fruit of the Spirit is love, joy, peace, longsuffering, gentleness, goodness, faith, meekness, temperance: against such there is no law."

- Galatians 5: 22, 23

"So that we may boldly say, The Lord *is* my helper, and I will not fear what man shall do unto me."

- Hebrews 13: 6

Chapter 39

The Grace of God

"ALSO unto thee, O Lord, *belongeth* mercy: for thou renderest to every man according to his work."

- Psalms 62: 12

"Let the field be joyful, and all that *is* therein: then shall all the trees of the wood rejoice Before the Lord: for he cometh, for he cometh to judge the earth: he shall judge the world with righteousness, and the people with his truth."

- Psalms 96: 12, 13

"But by the grace of God I am what I am: and his grace which *was bestowed* upon me was not in vain; but I laboured more abundantly than they all: yet not I, but the grace of God which was with me."

- 1 Corinthians 15: 10

"But unto every one of us is given grace according to the measure of the gift of Christ."

- Ephesians 4: 7

"In hope of eternal life, which God, *that* cannot lie, promised before the world began."

- Titus 1: 2

Chapter 40

The Whited Sepulchers

"FOR *there* is no faithfulness in their mouth; their inward part *is* very wickedness; their throat *is* an open sepulchre; they flatter with their tongue."

- Psalms 5: 9

"The harvest is the end of the world; and the reapers are the angels."

- Matthew 13: 39

"Woe unto you, scribes and Pharisees, hypocrites! for ye are like unto whited sepulchres, which indeed appear beautiful outward, but are within full of dead *men's* bones, and of all uncleanness."

- Matthew 23: 27

"Even so ye also outwardly appear righteous unto men, but within ye are full of hypocrisy and iniquity."

- Matthew 23: 28

"Having a form of godliness, but denying the power thereof: from such turn away."

- 2 Timothy 3: 5

"These are spots in your feasts of charity, when they feast with you, feeding themselves without fear: clouds *they are* without water, carried about of winds; trees whose fruit withereth, without fruit, twice dead, plucked up by the roots."

- Jude 1: 12

Chapter 41

The Temples of Ruin

"THOUGH they dig into hell, thence shall mine hand take them; though they climb up to heaven, thence will I bring them down."

- Amos 9: 2

"When the unclean spirit is gone out of a man, he walketh through dry places, seeking rest, and findeth none."

- Matthew 12: 43

"Then goeth he, and taketh with himself seven other spirits more wicked than himself, and they enter in and dwell there: and the last state of that man is worse than the first."

- Matthew 12: 45

"Know ye not that ye are the temple of God, and *that* the Spirit of God dwelleth in you?"

- 1 Corinthians 3: 16

"If any man defile the temple of God, him shall God destroy; for the temple of God is holy, which *temple* ye are."

- 1 Corinthians 3: 17

Chapter 42

The Valley of Bones

"THE sorrows of hell compassed me about; the snares of death prevented me."

- 2 Samuel 22: 6

"They have ears, but they hear not; neither is there *any* breath in their mouths."

- Psalms 135: 17

"Answer not a fool according to his folly, lest thou also be like unto him."

- Proverbs 26: 4

"The hand of the Lord was upon me, and carried me out in the spirit of the Lord, and set me down in the midst of the valley which *was* full of bones."

- Ezekiel 37: 1

"And caused me to pass by them round about: and, behold, *there were* very many in the open valley; and, lo, *they were* very dry."

- Ezekiel 37: 2

Chapter 43

The Living and the Dead

"AND he stood between the dead and the living, and the plague was stayed."

- Numbers 16: 48

"The dead praise not the Lord, neither any that go down into silence."

- Psalms 115: 17

"Follow me; and let the dead bury their dead."

- Matthew 8: 22

"But as touching the resurrection of the dead, have ye not read that which was spoken unto you by God, saying, I am the God of Abraham, and the God of Isaac, and the God of Jacob? God is not the God of the dead, but of the living."

- Matthew 22: 31, 32

"What went ye out to see? A reed shaken by the wind."

- Luke 7: 24

"Verily, verily, I say unto you, the hour is coming, and now is, when the dead shall hear the voice of the Son of God: and they that hear shall live."

- John 5: 25

Chapter 44

The Voice in the Wilderness

"WHOSO despiseth the word shall be destroyed: but he that feareth the commandment shall be rewarded."

- Proverbs 13: 13

"Until the spirit be poured upon us from on high, and the wilderness be a fruitful field, and the fruitful field be counted for a forest."

- Isaiah 32: 15

"The voice of him that crieth in the wilderness, Prepare ye the way of the Lord, make straight in the desert a highway for our God."

- Isaiah 40: 3

"Every valley shall be exalted, and every mountain and hill shall be made low; and the crooked shall be made straight, and the rough places plain."

- Isaiah 40: 4

"Thy holy cities are a wilderness, Zion is a wilderness, Jerusalem a desolation."

- Isaiah 64: 10

Chapter 45

The Barren Fields

"WOE unto them that join house to house, *that* lay field to field, till *there be* no place, that they may be placed alone in the midst of the earth!"

- Isaiah 5: 8

"The field is wasted, the land mourneth; for the corn is wasted: the new wine is dried up, the oil languisheth."

- Joel 1: 10

"Be ye ashamed, O ye husbandmen; howl, O ye vinedressers, for the wheat and for the barley; because the harvest of the field is perished."

- Joel 1: 11

"The seed is rotten under their clods, the garners are laid desolate, the barns are broken down; for the corn is withered."

- Joel 1: 17

"How do the beasts groan! the herds of cattle are perplexed, because they have no pasture; yea, the flocks of sheep are made desolate."

- Joel 1: 18

"O Lord, to thee will I cry: for the fire hath devoured the pastures of the wilderness, and the flame hath burned all the trees of the field."

- Joel 1: 19

"The beasts of the field cry also unto thee: for the rivers of waters are dried up, and the fire hath devoured the pastures of the wilderness."

- Joel 1: 20

"Then saith he to the man, Stretch forth thine hand. And he stretched *it* forth; and it was restored whole, like as the other."

- Matthew 12: 13

"The field is the world; the good seed are the children of the kingdom; but the tares are the children of the wicked *one*."

- Matthew 13: 38

"But the manifestation of the spirit is given to every man to profit withal."

- 1 Corinthians 12: 7

"Who shall change our vile body, that it may be fashioned like unto his glorious body, according to the working whereby he is able even to subdue all things unto himself."

- Philippians 3: 21

Chapter 46

The False Virtues

"HOW much then is a man better than a sheep? Wherefore it is lawful to do well on the sabbath days."

- Matthew 12: 12

"And be not conformed to this world: but be ye transformed by the renewing of your mind, that ye may prove what *is* that good, and acceptable, and perfect, will of God."

- Romans 12: 2

"For the wisdom of this world is foolishness with God. For it is written, He taketh the wise in their own craftiness."

- 1 Corinthians 3: 19

"(For many walk, of whom I have told you often, and now tell you even weeping, *that they are* the enemies of the cross of Christ: Whose end *is* destruction, whose God *is their* belly, and *whose* glory *is* in their shame, who mind earthly things.)"

- Philippians 3: 18, 19

"Be not forgetful to entertain strangers: for thereby some have entertained angels unawares."

- Hebrews 13: 2

Chapter 47

The False Values

"WHICH say to the seers, See not; and to the prophets, Prophesy not unto us right things, speak unto us smooth things, prophesy deceits."

- Isaiah 30: 10

"And judgment is turned away backward, and justice standeth afar off: for truth is fallen in the street, and equity cannot enter."

- Isaiah 59: 14

"As a cage is full of birds, so *are* their houses full of deceit: therefore they are become great, and waxen rich."

- Jeremiah 5: 27

"The prophets prophesy falsely, and the priests bear rule by their means; and my people love *to have it* so: and what will ye do in the end thereof?"

- Jeremiah 5: 31

"But if I live in the flesh, this *is* the fruit of my labour: yet what I shall choose I wot not."

- Philippians 1: 22

"Ye have lived in pleasure on the earth, and been wanton; ye have nourished yours hearts, as in a day of slaughter."

- James 5: 5

CHAPTER 48

THE PURE ADVANTAGE

"THEIR houses are safe from fear, neither *is* the rod of God upon them."

- Job 21: 9

"Blessed *are* the undefiled in the way, who walk in the law of the Lord."

- Psalms 119: 1

"Pleasant words *are as* an honeycomb, sweet to the soul, and health to the bones."

- Proverbs 16: 24

"That ye may be blameless and harmless, the sons of God, without rebuke, in the midst of a crooked and perverse nation, among whom ye shine as lights in the world."

- Philippians 2: 15

"To the end he may stablish your hearts unblameable in holiness before God, even our Father, at the coming of our Lord Jesus Christ with all his saints."

- 1 Thessalonians 3: 13

"Unto the pure all things *are* pure: but unto them that are defiled and unbelieving *is* nothing pure; but even their mind and conscience is defiled."

- Titus 1: 15

Chapter 49

The Absolution of Sin

"WHO can bring a clean *thing* out of an unclean? not one."

- Job 14: 4

"Neither do men put new wine into old bottles: else the bottles break, and the wine runneth out, and the bottles perish: but they put new wine into new bottles, and both are preserved."

- Matthew 9: 17

"And that ye put on the new man, which after God is created in righteousness and true holiness."

- Ephesians 4: 24

"Neither by the blood of goats and calves, but by his own blood he entered in once into the holy place, having obtained eternal redemption *for us*."

- Hebrews 9: 12

"We know that we have passed from death unto life, because we love the brethren. He that loveth not *his* brother abideth in death."

- 1 John 3: 14

"Remember therefore from whence thou art fallen, and repent, and do the first works; or else I will come unto thee quickly, and will remove thy candlestick out of his place, except thou repent."

- Revelation 2: 5

Chapter 50

The Pure Genius

"I UNDERSTAND more than the ancients, because I keep thy precepts."

- Psalms 119: 100

"The just *man* walketh in his integrity: his children *are* blessed after him."

- Proverbs 20: 7

"Even so every good tree bringeth forth good fruit; but a corrupt tree bringeth forth evil fruit."

- Matthew 7: 17

"A good tree cannot bring forth evil fruit, neither can a corrupt tree bring forth good fruit."

- Matthew 7: 18

"He that soweth the good seed is the Son of man."

- Matthew 13: 37

Chapter 51

The Moderate Man

"AND put a knife to thy throat, if thou *be* a man given to appetite."

- Proverbs 23: 2

"All the labour of man *is* for his mouth, and yet the appetite is not filled."

- Ecclesiastes 6: 7

"For he that eateth and drinketh unworthily, eateth and drinketh damnation to himself, not discerning the Lord's body."

- 1 Corinthians 11: 29

"For this cause many *are* weak and sickly among you, and many sleep."

- 1 Corinthians 11: 30

"Let your moderation be known unto all men. The Lord *is* at hand."

- Philippians 4: 5

Chapter 52

The Eternal Treasure

"THE idols of the heathen *are* silver and gold, the work of men's hands."

- Psalms 135: 15

"Treasures of wickedness profit nothing: but righteousness delivereth from death."

- Proverbs 10: 2

"Wise *men* lay up knowledge: but the mouth of the foolish *is* near destruction."

- Proverbs 10: 14

"For where your treasure is, there will your heart be also."

- Luke 12: 34

"That the trial of your faith, being much more precious than of gold that perisheth."

- 1 Peter 1: 7

"Love not the world, neither the things *that are* in the world. If any man love the world, the love of the Father is not in him."

- 1 John 2: 15

Chapter 53

The Will of Man

"HE that walketh uprightly walketh surely: but he that perverteth his ways shall be known."

- Proverbs 10: 9

"*There are* many devices in a man's heart; nevertheless the counsel of the Lord, that shall stand."

- Proverbs 19: 21

"The highways lie waste, the wayfaring man ceaseth: he hath broken the covenant, he hath despised the cities, he regardeth no man."

- Isaiah 33: 8

"And the rain descended, and the floods came, and the winds blew, and beat upon the house; and it fell: and great was the fall of it."

- Matthew 7: 27

"For that ye *ought* to say, If the Lord will, we shall live, and do this, or that."

- James 4: 15

Chapter 54

The Will of God

"THE fear of the Lord *tendeth* to life: and *he that hath it* shall abide satisfied; he shall not be visited with evil."

- Proverbs 19: 23

"And all the inhabitants of the earth *are* reputed as nothing: and he doeth according to his will in the army of heaven, and *among* the inhabitants of the earth: and none can stay his hand, or say unto him, What doest thou?"

- Daniel 4: 35

"Be ye therefore perfect, even as your Father which is in heaven is perfect."

- Matthew 5: 48

"Not every one that saith unto me, Lord, Lord, shall enter into the kingdom of heaven; but he that doeth the will of my Father which is in heaven."

- Matthew 7: 21

"Behold, I shew you a mystery; We shall not all sleep, but we shall all be changed."

- 1 Corinthians 15: 51

Chapter 55

🌾 The Finite Mind 🌾

"MAN'S goings *are* of the Lord; how can a man then understand his own way?"

- Proverbs 20: 24

"*Be* of the same mind one toward another. Mind not high things, but condescend to men of low estate. Be not wise in your own conceits."

- Romans 12: 16

"Now I beseech you, brethren, by the name of our Lord Jesus Christ, that ye all speak the same thing, and *that* there be no divisions among you; but *that* ye be perfectly joined together in the same mind and in the same judgment."

- 1 Corinthians 1: 10

"Fulfill ye my joy, that ye be likeminded, having the same love, *being* of one accord, of one mind."

- Philippians 2: 2

Chapter 56

The Infinite Mind

"LET us pass, I pray thee, through thy country: we will not pass through the fields, or through the vineyards, neither will we drink *of* the water of the wells: we will go by the king's *high* way, we will not turn to the right hand nor to the left, until we have passed thy borders."

- Numbers 20: 17

"*Is* not thy wickedness great? and thine iniquities infinite?"

- Job 22: 5

"He shall have dominion also from sea to sea, and from the river unto the ends of the earth."

- Psalms 72: 8

"Great *is* our Lord, and of great power: his understanding *is* infinite."

- Psalms 147: 5

"They shall not hurt nor destroy in all my holy mountain; for the earth shall be full of the knowledge of the Lord, as the waters cover the sea."

- Isaiah 11: 9

Chapter 57

The Spiral Staircase

"AND he dreamed, and behold a ladder set up on the earth, and the top of it reached to heaven: and behold the angels of God ascending and descending on it."

- Genesis 28: 12

"And behold, the Lord stood above it, and said, I *am* the Lord God of Abraham thy father, and the God of Isaac: the land whereon thou liest, to thee will I give it, and to thy seed."

- Genesis 28: 13

"And thy seed shall be as the dust of the earth, and thou shalt spread abroad to the west, and to the east, and to the north, and to the south: and in thee and in thy seed shall all the families of the earth be blessed."

- Genesis 28: 14

"And behold, I *am* with thee, and will keep thee in all *places* whither thou goest, and will bring thee again into this land; for I will not leave thee, until I have done *that* which I have spoken to thee of."

- Genesis 28: 15

"And Jacob awaked out of his sleep, and he said, Surely the Lord is in this place; and I knew *it* not."

- Genesis 28: 16

"And he was afraid, and said, How dreadful *is* this place! this *is* none other but the house of God, and this *is* the gate of heaven."

- Genesis 28: 17

"They mount up to the heaven, they go down again to the depths: their soul is melted because of trouble."

- Psalms 107: 26

"If I ascend up into heaven, thou *art* there: if I make my bed in hell, behold, thou *art there*."

- Psalms 139: 8

"For which of you, intending to build a tower, sitteth not down first, and counteth the cost, whether he have *sufficient* to finish *it*?"

- Luke 14: 28

Chapter 58

The Positive and Negative

"ALL the days of the afflicted *are* evil: but he that is of a merry heart *hath* a continual feast."

- Proverbs 15: 15

"But the ship was now in the midst of the sea, tossed with waves: for the wind was contrary."

- Matthew 14: 24

"For the flesh lusteth against the Spirit, and the Spirit against the flesh: and these are contrary the one to the other: so that ye cannot do the things that ye would."

- Galatians 5: 17

"But strong meat belongeth to them that are of full age, *even* those who by reason of use have their senses exercised to discern both good and evil."

- Hebrews 5: 14

"Not rendering evil for evil, or railing for railing: but contrariwise blessing; knowing that ye are thereunto called, that ye should inherit a blessing."

- 1 Peter 3: 9

Chapter 59

The Burden of Density

"THE Lord *is* far from the wicked: but he heareth the prayer of the righteous."

- Proverbs 15: 29

"Wherefore he saith, When he ascended up on high, he led captivity captive, and gave gifts unto men."

- Ephesians 4: 8

"(Now that he ascended, what is it but that he also descended first into the lower parts of the earth?"

- Ephesians 4: 9

"He that descended is the same also that ascended up far above all heavens, that he might fill all things.)"

- Ephesians 4: 10

Chapter 60

The Planes of Desire

"THE desire accomplished is sweet to the soul: but *it is* abomination to fools to depart from evil."

- Proverbs 13: 19

"But woe unto you, scribes and Pharisees, hypocrites! for ye shut up the kingdom of heaven against men: for ye neither go in *yourselves*; neither suffer ye them that are entering to go in."

- Matthew 23: 13

"And there sat a certain man at Lystra, impotent in his feet, being a cripple from his mother's womb, who never had walked."

- Acts 14: 8

"And have no fellowship with the unfruitful works of darkness, but rather reprove *them*."

- Ephesians 5: 11

"And make straight paths for your feet, lest that which is lame be turned out of the way; but let it rather be healed."

- Hebrews 12: 13

"This wisdom descendeth not from above, but *is* earthly, sensual, devilish."

- James 3: 15

Chapter 61

The Scales of Justice

"THERE shall no evil happen to the just: but the wicked shall be filled with mischief."

- Proverbs 12: 21

"Evil pursueth sinners: but to the righteous good shall be repayed."

- Proverbs 13: 21

"But a certain fearful looking for of judgment and fiery indignation, which shall devour the adversaries."

- Hebrews 10: 27

"For we know him that hath said, Vengeance *belongeth* unto me, I will recompense, saith the Lord, And again, The Lord shall judge his people."

- Hebrews 10: 30

"*It is* a fearful thing to fall into the hands of the living God."

- Hebrews 10: 31

CHAPTER 62

THE WAVES OF KARMA

"WHEN the waves of death compassed me, the floods of ungodly men made me afraid."

- 2 Samuel 22: 5

"The Lord sitteth upon the flood; yea, the Lord sitteth King for ever."

- Psalms 28: 10

"Thou carriest them away as with a flood..."

- Psalms 90: 5

"A good *man* leaveth an inheritance to his children's children: and the wealth of the sinner *is* laid up for the just."

- Proverbs 13: 22

"And after threescore and two weeks shall Messiah be cut off, but not for himself: and the people of the prince that shall come shall destroy the city and the sanctuary; and the end thereof *shall be* with a flood, and unto the end of the war desolations are determined."

- Daniel 9: 26

"In these lay a great multitude of impotent folk, of blind, halt, withered, waiting for the moving of the water."

- John 5: 3

Chapter 63

The Crucible of Time

"MY times *are* in thy hand: deliver me from the hand of mine enemies, and from them that persecute me."

- Psalms 31: 15

"To every *thing there is* a season, and a time to every purpose under the heaven."

- Ecclesiastes 3: 1

"A time to be born, and a time to die; a time to plant, and a time to pluck up *that which is* planted."

- Ecclesiastes 3: 2

"A time to kill, and a time to heal; a time to break down, and a time to build up."

- Ecclesiastes 3: 3

"A time to weep, and a time to laugh; a time to mourn, and a time to dance."

- Ecclesiastes 3: 4

"A time to cast away stones, and a time to gather stones together; a time to embrace, and a time to refrain from embracing."

- Ecclesiastes 3: 5

"A time to get, and a time to lose; a time to keep, and a time to cast away."

- Ecclesiastes 3: 6

"A time to rend, and a time to sew; a time to keep silence, and a time to speak."

- Ecclesiastes 3: 7

"A time to love, and a time to hate; a time of war, and a time of peace."

- Ecclesiastes 3: 8

"For *it is* the day of the Lord's vengeance, *and* the year of recompences for the controversy of Zion."

- Isaiah 34: 8

Chapter 64

The Inexperienced Man

"*IT is* good for me that I have been afflicted; that I might learn thy statutes."

- Psalms 119: 71

"He that walketh with wise *men* shall be wise: but a companion of fools shall be destroyed."

- Proverbs 13: 20

"An instructor of the foolish, a teacher of babes, which hast the form of knowledge and of the truth in the law."

- Romans 2: 20

"And I, brethren, could not speak unto you as unto spiritual, but as unto carnal, *even* as unto babes in Christ."

- 1 Corinthians 3: 1

"I have fed you with milk, and not with meat: for hitherto ye were not able *to bear it*, neither yet now are ye able."

- 1 Corinthians 3: 2

"For ye are yet carnal: for whereas *there is* among you envying, and strife, and divisions, are ye not carnal, and walk as men?"

- 1 Corinthians 3: 3

Chapter 65

The Experienced Man

"A PRUDENT man concealeth knowledge: but the heart of fools proclaimeth foolishness."

- Proverbs 12: 23

"The law of the wise *is* a fountain of life, to depart from the snares of death."

- Proverbs 13: 14

"And he gave some, apostles; and some, prophets; and some, evangelists; and some, pastors and teachers."

- Ephesians 4: 11

"For the perfecting of the saints, for the work of the ministry, for the edifying of the body of Christ."

- Ephesians 4: 12

"Till we all come in the unity of the faith, and of the knowledge of the Son of God, unto a perfect man, unto the measure of the stature of the fullness of Christ."

- Ephesians 4: 13

Chapter 66

The Immature Soul

"REMEMBER not the sins of my youth, nor my transgressions: according to thy mercy remember thou me for thy goodness' sake, O Lord."

- Psalms 25: 7

"Learn to do well, seek judgment, relieve the oppressed, judge the fatherless, plead for the widow."

- Isaiah 1: 17

"Let no man deceive himself. If any man among you seemeth to be wise in this world, let him become a fool, that he may be wise."

- 1 Corinthians 3: 18

"Wherefore seeing we also are compassed about with so great a cloud of witnesses, let us lay aside every weight, and the sin which doth so easily beset *us*, and let us run with patience the race that is set before us."

- Hebrews 12: 1

Chapter 67

The Mature Soul

"WISDOM hath builded her house, she hath hewn out her seven pillars."

- Proverbs 9: 1

"She hath killed her beasts; she hath mingled her wine; she hath also furnished her table."

- Proverbs 9: 2

"Whoso *is* simple, let him turn in hither: *as for* him that wanteth understanding, she saith to him."

- Proverbs 9: 4

"Come, eat of my bread, and drink of the wine *which* I have mingled."

- Proverbs 9: 5

"Forsake the foolish, and live; and go in the way of understanding."

- Proverbs 9: 6

"The fear of the Lord *is* the beginning of wisdom: and the knowledge of the holy *is* understanding."

- Proverbs 9: 10

"Butter and honey shall he eat, that he may know to refuse the evil, and choose the good."

- Isaiah 7: 15

CHAPTER 68

THE SACRED SOUND

"*LET* the high *praises* of God *be* in their mouth, and a twoedged sword in their hand."

- Psalms 149: 6

"The song of songs..."

- The Song of Solomon 1: 1

"From the sole of the foot even unto the head *there is* no soundness in it; *but* wounds, and bruises, and putrifying sores..."

- Isaiah 1: 6

"And he shall send his angels with a great sound of a trumpet, and they shall gather together his elect from the four winds, from one end of heaven to the other."

- Matthew 24: 31

"The wind bloweth where it listeth, and thou hearest the sound thereof, but canst not tell whence it cometh, and whither it goeth: so is every one that is born of the spirit."

- John 3: 8

"But I say, Have they not heard? Yes verily, their sound went into all the earth, and their words unto the ends of the world."

- Romans 10: 18

Chapter 69

The Stir of Enchantment

"NEITHER shall ye use enchantment, nor observe times."

- Leviticus 19: 26

"Hell from beneath is moved for thee to meet *thee* at thy coming: it stirreth up the dead for thee, *even* all the chief ones of the earth; it hath raised up from their thrones all the kings of the nations."

- Isaiah 14: 9

"I therefore, the prisoner of the Lord, beseech you that ye walk worthy of the vocation wherewith ye are called."

- Ephesians 4: 1

"With all lowliness and meekness, with longsuffering, forbearing one another in love."

- Ephesians 4: 2

"Wherefore I put thee in remembrance that thou stir up the gift of God, which is in thee by the putting on of my hands."

- 2 Timothy 1: 6

"Yea, I think it meet, as long as I am in this tabernacle, to stir you up by putting *you* in remembrance."

- 2 Peter 1: 13

Chapter 70

The Unnatural Mind

"OF the rock *that* begat thee thou art unmindful, and hast forgotten God that formed thee."

- Deuteronomy 32: 18

"Whose hope shall be cut off, and whose trust *shall be* a spider's web."

- Job 8: 14

"My days are past, my purposes are broken off, *even* the thoughts of my heart."

- Job 17: 11

"I am forgotten as a dead man out of mind: I am like a broken vessel."

- Psalms 31: 12

"They reel to and fro, and stagger like a drunken man, and are at their wits' end."

- Psalms 107: 27

"And they shall turn away *their* ears from the truth, and shall be turned unto fables."

- 2 Timothy 4: 4

Chapter 71

The Wheel of Mind

"TERRORS shall make him afraid on every side, and shall drive him to his feet."

- Job 18: 11

"Then they cry unto the Lord in their trouble, and he bringeth them out of their distresses."

- Psalms 107: 28

"The fear of man bringeth a snare: but whoso putteth his trust in the Lord shall be safe."

- Proverbs 29: 25

"Sanctify the Lord of hosts himself; and *let* him *be* your fear, and *let* him *be* your dread."

- Isaiah 8: 13

"And be renewed in the spirit of your mind."

- Ephesians 4: 23

"Behold also the great ships, which though *they be* so great, and *are* driven of fierce winds, yet are they turned about with a very small helm, whithersoever the governor listeth."

- James 3: 4

Chapter 72

The Natural Mind

"BE ye mindful always of his covenant; the word *which* he commanded to a thousand generations."

- 1 Chronicles 16: 15

"He maketh the storm a calm, so that the waves thereof are still."

- Psalms 107: 29

"They that be whole need not a physician, but they that are sick."

- Matthew 9: 12

"Endeavouring to keep the unity of the Spirit in the bond of peace."

- Ephesians 4: 3

"For God hath not given us the spirit of fear; but of power, and of love, and of a sound mind."

- 2 Timothy 1: 7

"In meekness instructing those that oppose themselves; if God peradventure will give them repentance to the acknowledging of the truth."

- 2 Timothy 3: 25

Chapter 73

The Turnabout

"HE hath fenced up my way that I cannot pass, and he hath set darkness in my paths."

- Job 19: 8

"Turn us again, O God, and cause thy face to shine; and we shall be saved."

- Psalms 80: 3

"Poverty and shame *shall be to* him that refuseth instruction: but he that regardeth reproof shall be honoured."

- Proverbs 13: 18

"For thus saith the Lord God, the Holy One of Israel; In returning and rest shall ye be saved; in quietness and in confidence shall be your strength: and ye would not."

- Isaiah 30: 15

"Cast away from you all your transgressions, whereby ye have transgressed; and make you a new heart and a new spirit: for why will ye die, O house of Israel?"

- Ezekiel 18: 31

"For I have no pleasure in the death of him that dieth, saith the Lord God: wherefore turn *yourselves*, and live ye."

- Ezekiel 18: 32

Chapter 74

The Separation

"NOW therefore make confession unto the Lord God of your fathers, and do his pleasure: and separate yourselves from the people of the land, and from the strange wives."

- Ezra 10: 11

"Why do the heathen rage, and the people imagine a vain thing?"

- Psalms 2: 1

"Behold, all souls are mine; as the soul of the father, so also the soul of the son is mine: the soul that sinneth, it shall die."

- Ezekiel 18: 4

"Wherefore come out from among them, and be ye separate, saith the Lord, and touch not the unclean *thing*; and I will receive you."

- 2 Corinthians 6: 17

"Casting down imaginations, and every high thing that exalteth itself against the knowledge of God, and bringing into captivity every thought to the obedience of Christ."

- 2 Corinthians 10: 5

"For while envying and strife *is*, there *is* confusion and every evil work."

- James 3: 16

Chapter 75

The Separate Self

"FOR whosoever will save his life shall lose it: and whosoever will lose his life for my sake shall find it."

- Matthew 16: 25

"And he said, This will I do: I will pull down my barns, and build greater; and there will I bestow all my fruits and my goods."

- Luke 12: 18

"And I will to my soul, Soul, thou hast much goods laid up for many years; take thine ease, eat, drink, *and* be merry."

- Luke 12: 19

"But God said unto him, *Thou* fool, this night thy soul shall be required of thee: then whose shall those things be, which thou hast provided."

- Luke 12: 20

"So *is* he that layeth up treasure for himself, and is not rich toward God."

- Luke 12: 21

"Whom the heaven must receive until the times of restitution of all things, which God hath spoken by the mouth of all his holy prophets since the world began."

- Acts 3: 21

Chapter 76

The Microcosmic Self

"FOR *in* six days the Lord made heaven and earth, the sea, and all that in them *is*, and rested the seventh day: wherefore the Lord blessed the sabbath day, and hallowed it."

- Exodus 20: 11

"Let the heaven and earth praise him, the seas, and every thing that moveth therein."

- Psalms 69: 34

"*So is* this great and wide sea, wherein *are* things creeping innumerable, both small and great beasts."

- Psalms 104: 25

"So we, *being* many, are one body in Christ, and every one members one of another."

- Romans 12: 5

"Moreover, brethren, I would not that ye should be ignorant, how that all our fathers were under the cloud, and all passed through the sea."

- 1 Corinthians 10: 1

"For the body is not one member, but many."

- 1 Corinthians 12: 14

Chapter 77

The Macrocosmic Self

"LET the sea roar, and the fullness thereof: let the fields rejoice, and all that *is* therein."

- 1 Chronicles 16: 32

"For ye are bought with a price: therefore glorify God in your body, and in your spirit, which are God's."

- 1 Corinthians 6: 20

"*There is* one body, and one Spirit, even as ye are called in one hope of your calling."

- Ephesians 4: 4

"One Lord, one faith, one baptism."

- Ephesians 4: 5

"One God and Father of all, who *is* above all, and through all, and in you all."

- Ephesians 4: 6

Chapter 78

 The Master's Vessel

"THOU hast been faithful over a few things, I will make thee ruler over many things."

- Matthew 25: 23

"And said unto them, Sirs, I perceive that this voyage will be with hurt and much damage, not only of the lading and ship, but also of our lives."

- Acts 27: 10

"And when the ship was caught, and could not bear up into the wind, we let *her* drive."

- Acts 27: 15

"And now I exhort you to be of good cheer: for there shall be no loss of *any man's* life among you, but of the ship."

- Acts 27: 22

"From whom the whole body fitly joined together and compacted by that which every joint supplieth, according to the effectual working in the measure of every part, maketh increase of the body unto the edifying of itself in love."

- Ephesians 4: 16

THE MASTER

"AND, behold, God himself *is* with us for *our* captain, and his priests with sounding trumpets to cry alarm against you. O children of Israel, fight ye not against the Lord God of your fathers; for ye shall not prosper."

- 2 Chronicles 13: 12

"In that day will I raise up the tabernacle of David that is fallen, and close up the breaches thereof; and I will raise up his ruins, and I will build it as in the days of old."

- Amos 9: 11

"That we *henceforth* be no more children, tossed to and fro, and carried about with every wind of doctrine, by the sleight of men, *and* cunning craftiness, whereby they lie in wait to deceive."

- Ephesians 4: 14

"But speaking the truth in love, may grow up into him in all things, which is the head, even Christ."

- Ephesians 4: 15

"And without controversy great is the mystery of godliness: God was manifest in the flesh, justified in the Spirit, seen by angels, preached unto the gentiles, believed on in the world, received up into glory."

- 1 Timothy 3: 16

Chapter 80

The Assessment

"THERE is none holy as the Lord: for *there is* none beside thee: neither *is there* any rock like our God."

- 1 Samuel 2: 2

"Talk no more so exceeding proudly; let *not* arrogancy come out of your mouth: for the Lord *is* a God of knowledge, and by him actions are weighed."

- 1 Samuel 2: 3

"The bows of the mighty men *are* broken, and they that stumbled are girded with strength."

- 1 Samuel 2: 4

"And we being exceedingly tossed with a tempest, the next *day* they lightened the ship."

- Acts 27: 18

"For I reckon that the sufferings of this present time *are* not worthy *to be compared* with the glory which shall be revealed in us."

- Romans 8: 18

"And this *word,* Yet once more, signifieth the removing of those things that are shaken, as of things that are made, that those things which cannot be shaken may remain."

- Hebrews 12: 27

Chapter 81

The Mortal Grid

"FOR this corruptible must put on incorruption, and this mortal *must* put on immortality."

- 1 Corinthians 15: 53

"For we know that if our earthly house of *this* tabernacle were dissolved, we have a building of God, an house not made with hands, eternal in the heavens."

- 2 Corinthians 5: 1

"For in this we groan, earnestly desiring to be clothed upon with our house which is from heaven."

- 2 Corinthians 5: 2

"If so be that being clothed we shall not be found naked."

- 2 Corinthians 5: 3

"For we that are in *this* tabernacle do groan, being burdened: not for that we would be unclothed, but clothed upon, that mortality might be swallowed up of life."

- 2 Corinthians 5: 4

"*Seeing* then *that* all these things shall be dissolved, what manner *of persons* ought ye to be in *all* holy conversation and godliness."

- 2 Peter 3: 11

Chapter 82

The Immortal Grid

"ART thou the first man *that* was born? or wast thou made before the hills?"

- Job 15: 7

"These see the works of the Lord, and his wonders in the deep."

- Psalms 107: 24

"But is now made manifest by the appearing of our Saviour Jesus Christ, who hath abolished death, and hath brought life and immortality to light through the gospel."

- 2 Timothy 1: 10

"Through faith we understand that the worlds were framed by the word of God, so that things which are seen were not made of things which do appear."

- Hebrews 11: 3

Chapter 83

The Puzzle

"BUT where shall wisdom be found? and where *is* the place of understanding?"

- Job 28: 12

"Man knoweth not the price thereof; neither is it found in the land of the living."

- Job 28: 13

"The depth saith, It *is* not in me: and the sea saith, *It is* not with me."

- Job 28: 14

"For he looketh to the ends of the earth, *and* seeth under the whole heaven."

- Job 28: 24

"Then did he see it, and declare it; he prepared it, yea, and searched it out."

- Job 28: 27

"And unto man he said, Behold, the fear of the Lord, that *is* wisdom; and to depart from evil *is* understanding."

- Job 28: 28

Chapter 84

The Message

"A WICKED messenger falleth into mischief: but a faithful ambassador *is* health."

- Proverbs 13: 17

"The highway of the upright *is* to depart from evil: he that keepeth his way preserveth his soul."

- Proverbs 16: 17

"Then said Jesus unto his disciples, If any *man* will come after me, let him deny himself, and take up his cross, and follow me."

- Matthew 16: 24

"For when for the time ye ought to be teachers, ye have need that one teach you again which *be* the first principles of the oracles of God; and are become such as have need of milk, and not of strong meat."

- Hebrews 5: 12

"He that saith he abideth in him ought himself also so to walk, even as he walked."

- 1 John 1: 6

Chapter 85

The Messenger

"FOR the word of the Lord *is* right; and all his works *are done* in truth."

- Psalms 33: 4

"Behold, I will send my messenger, and he shall prepare the way before me: and the Lord, whom ye seek, shall suddenly come to his temple, even the messenger of the covenant, whom ye delight in: behold, he shall come, saith the Lord of hosts."

- Malachi 3: 1

"I must work the works of him that sent me, while it is day: the night cometh, when no man can work."

- John 9: 4

"Whereunto I am appointed a preacher, and an apostle, and a teacher of the gentiles."

- 2 Timothy 1: 11

"And being made perfect, he became the author of eternal salvation unto all them that obey him."

- Hebrews 5: 9

"For there are three that bear record in heaven, the Father, the Word, and the Holy Ghost: and these three are one."

- 1 John 5: 7

Chapter 86

The Rigid

"THEIR soul abhorreth all manner of meat; and they draw near unto the gates of death."

- Psalms 107: 18

"Every prudent *man* dealeth with knowledge: but a fool layeth open *his* folly."

- Proverbs 13: 16

"For I bear them record that they have a zeal of God, but not according to knowledge."

- Romans 10: 2

"In all things shewing thyself a pattern of good works: in doctrine *shewing* uncorruptness, gravity, sincerity."

- Titus 2: 7

"But avoid foolish questions, and genealogies, and contentions, and strivings about the law; for they are unprofitable and vain."

- Titus 3: 9

"As newborn babes, desire the sincere milk of the word, that ye may grow thereby."

- 1 Peter 2: 2

Chapter 87

The Fearful

"AND the serpent said unto the woman, Ye shall not surely die."

- Genesis 3: 4

"The fear of the wicked, it shall come upon him: but the desire of the righteous shall be granted."

- Proverbs 10: 24

"But your iniquities have separated between you and your God, and your sins have hid *his* face from you, that he will not hear."

- Isaiah 59: 2

"Walk in the fear of the Lord and in the comfort of the Holy Spirit."

- Acts 9: 31

"Wherefore, as by one man sin entereth into the world, and death by sin; and so death passed upon all men, for that all have sinned."

- Romans 5: 12

"And I say unto you my friends, Be not afraid of them that kill the body, and after that have no more that they can do."

- Luke 12: 4

"But I will forewarn you whom ye shall fear: Fear him, which after he hath killed hath power to cast into hell; yea, I say unto you, Fear him."

- Luke 12: 5

Chapter 88

The Day of Judgment

"LET the sinners be consumed out of the earth, and let the wicked be no more. Bless thou the Lord, O my soul, Praise ye the Lord."

- Psalms 104: 35

"And now also the axe is laid unto the root of the trees: therefore every tree which bringeth not forth good fruit is hewn down, and cast into the fire."

- Matthew 3: 10

"For there is nothing covered, that shall not be revealed; neither hid, that shall not be known."

- Luke 12: 2

"But the day of the Lord will come as a thief in the night; in the which the heavens shall pass away with a great noise, and the elements shall melt with fervent heat, the earth also and the works that are therein shall be burned up."

- 2 Peter 3: 10

"And the stars of heaven fell unto the earth, even as a fig tree casteth her untimely figs, when she is shaken of a mighty wind."

- Revelation 6: 13

"And the heaven departed as a scroll when it is rolled together; and every mountain and island were moved out of their places."

- Revelation 6: 14

Chapter 89

The Day of Desolation

"SHALL thy lovingkindness be declared in the grave? *or* thy faithfulness in destruction?"

- Psalms 88: 11

"When your fear cometh as desolation, and your destruction cometh as a whirlwind; when distress and anguish cometh upon you."

- Proverbs 1: 27

"Then shall they call upon me, but I will not answer; they shall seek me early, but they shall not find me."

- Proverbs 1: 28

"Awake, ye drunkards, and weep; and howl, all ye drinkers of wine, because of the new wine; for it is cut off from your mouth."

- Joel 1: 5

"He hath laid my vine waste, and barked my fig tree: he hath made it clean bare, and cast *it* away; the branches thereof are made white. Lament like a virgin girded with sackcloth for the husband of her youth."

- Joel 1: 7, 8

"For *in* those days shall be affliction, such as was not from the beginning of the creation which God created unto this time, neither shall be."

- Mark 13: 19

Chapter 90

The Evildoer and the Liar

"HE that worketh deceit shall not dwell within my house: he that telleth lies shall not tarry in my sight."

- Psalms 101: 7

"He becometh poor that dealeth *with* a slack hand: but the hand of the diligent maketh rich."

- Proverbs 10: 4

"Lying lips *are* abomination to the Lord: but they that deal truly *are* his delight."

- Proverbs 12: 22

"Whoso causeth the righteous to go astray in an evil way, he shall fall himself into his own pit..."

- Proverbs 28: 10

"That this *is* a rebellious people, lying children, children *that* will not hear the law of the Lord."

- Isaiah 30: 9

"And they shall pollute the sanctuary of strength, and shall take away the daily *sacrifice*, and they shall place the abomination that maketh desolate."

- Daniel 11: 31

"O generation of vipers, how can ye, being evil, speak good things? For out of the abundance of the heart the mouth speaketh."

- Matthew 12: 34

"When ye therefore shall see the abomination of desolation, spoken of by Daniel the prophet, stand in the holy place, (whoso readeth, let him understand.)"

- Matthew 24: 15

"Not slothful in business..."

- Romans 12: 11

"But evil men and seducers shall wax worse and worse, deceiving, and being deceived."

- 2 Timothy 3: 13

"They profess that they know God; but in works they deny *him*, being abominable, and disobedient, and unto every good work reprobate."

- Titus 1: 16

"Who is a liar but he hat denieth that Jesus is the Christ? He is antichrist, that denieth the Father and the Son."

- 1 John 2: 22

"For many deceivers are entered into the world, who confess not that Jesus Christ is come in the flesh. This is a deceiver and an antichrist."

- 2 John 1: 7

Chapter 91

The Blessing and the Curse

"AND afterward he read all the words of the law, the blessings and cursings, according to all that is written in the book of the law."

- Joshua 8: 34

"But this people who knoweth not the law are cursed."

- John 7: 49

"Am I therefore become your enemy, because I tell you the truth."

- Galatians 4: 16

"Alexander the coppersmith did me much evil: the Lord reward him according to his works."

- 2 Timothy 4: 14

"Neither is there any creature that is not manifest in his sight: but all things *are* naked and opened unto the eyes of him with whom we have to do."

- Hebrews 4: 13

Chapter 92

The True Israelite

"THE law of his God *is* in his heart; none of his steps shall slide."

- Psalms 37: 31

"But they shall sit every man under his vine and under his fig tree; and none shall make *them* afraid: for the mouth of the Lord of hosts hath spoken *it*."

- Micah 4: 4

"Ye are the light of the world. A city that is set on an hill cannot be hid."

- Matthew 5: 14

"*And* we know that we are of God, and the whole world lieth in wickedness."

- 1 John 5: 19

"These are they which were not defiled with women; for they are virgins. These are they which follow the Lamb whithersoever he goeth. These were redeemed from among men, *being* the firstfruits unto God and to the Lamb."

- Revelation 14: 4

"And in their mouth was found no guile: for they are without fault before the throne of God."

- Revelation 14: 5

Chapter 93

# The Discriminator

"MY father peradventure will feel me, and I shall seem to him as a deceiver; and I shall bring a curse upon me, and not a blessing."

- Genesis 27: 12

"A virtuous woman *is* a crown to her husband: but she that maketh ashamed *is* as rottenness in his bones."

- Proverbs 12: 4

"The eyes of the Lord *are* in every place, beholding the evil and the good."

- Proverbs 15: 3

"Wherefore by their fruits ye shall know them."

- Matthew 7: 20

"He spake also this parable; A certain *man* had a fig tree planted in his vineyard; and he came and sought fruit thereon, and found none."

- Luke 13: 6

"That they should seek the Lord, if haply they might feel after him, and find him, though he be not far from every one of us."

- Acts 17: 27

Chapter 94

The Division

"THINK not that I am come to send peace on Earth: I came not to send peace, but a sword."

- Matthew 10: 34

"And before him shall be gathered all nations; and he shall separate them one from another, as a shepherd divideth *his* sheep from the goats."

- Matthew 25: 32

"For first of all, when ye come together in the church, I hear that there be divisions among you; and I partly believe it."

- 1 Corinthians 11: 18

"Study to shew thyself approved unto God, a workman that needeth not to be ashamed, rightly dividing the word of truth."

- 2 Timothy 2: 15

"For the word of God *is* quick, and powerful, and sharper than any two-edged sword, piercing even to the dividing asunder of soul and spirit, and of the joints and marrow, and *is* a discerner of the thoughts and intents of the heart."

- Hebrews 4: 12

CHAPTER 95

THE SWORD OF TRUTH

"BE ye afraid of the sword: for wrath *bringeth* the punishments of the sword, that ye may know *there is* a judgment."

- Job 19: 29

"It is the spirit that quickeneth; the flesh profiteth nothing: the words that I speak unto you, *they* are spirit, and *they* are life."

- John 6: 63

"Sound speech, that cannot be condemned; that he that is of the contrary part may be ashamed, having no evil thing to say of you."

- Titus 2: 8

"A man that is an heretick after the first and second admonition reject."

- Titus 3: 10

"Knowing that he that is such is subverted, and sinneth, being condemned of himself."

- Titus 3: 11

"And out of his mouth goeth a sharp sword, that with it he should smite the nations: and he shall rule them with a rod of iron: and he treadeth the winepress of the fierceness and wrath of Almighty God."

- Revelation 19: 15

Chapter 96

The Hardened

"HARDEN not your heart, as in the provocation, *and* as *in* the day of temptation in the wilderness."

- Psalms 95: 8

"He hath blinded their eyes, and hardened their heart; that they should not see with *their* eyes, nor understand with *their* heart, and be converted, and I should hear them."

- John 12: 40

"Because that, when they knew God, they glorified *him* not as God, neither were thankful; but became vain in their imaginations, and their foolish heart was darkened."

- Romans 1: 21

"But exhort one another daily, while it is called To day; lest any of you be hardened through the deceitfulness of sin."

- Hebrews 3: 13

"For here we have no continuing city, but we seek one to come."

- Hebrews 13: 14

Chapter 97

The Needful

"FOR the Lord heareth the poor, and despiseth not his prisoners."

- Psalms 69: 33

"He will regard the prayer of the destitute, and not despise their prayer."

- Psalms 102: 17

"The Lord will not suffer the soul of the righteous to famish: but he casteth away the substance of the wicked."

- Proverbs 10: 3

"Nevertheless to abide in the flesh *is* more needful for you."

- Philippians 1: 24

"But whoso hath this world's good, and seeth his brother have need, and shutteth up his bowels *of compassion* from him, how dwelleth the love of God in him."

- 1 John 3: 17

Chapter 98

The Abusers

"WHOSO robbeth his father or his mother, and saith, *It is* no transgression; the same *is* the companion of a destroyer."

- Proverbs 28: 24

"And they that use this world, as not abusing *it*: for the fashion of this world passeth away."

- 1 Corinthians 7: 31

"But we know that the law *is* good, if a man use it lawfully."

- 1 Timothy 1: 8

"And there appeared a great wonder in heaven; a woman clothed with the sun, and the moon under her feet, and upon her head a crown of twelve stars."

- Revelation 12: 1

"And she being with child cried, travailing in birth, and pained to be delivered."

- Revelation 12: 2

Chapter 99

The Stream

"HE turneth rivers into a wilderness, and the watersprings into dry ground."

- Psalms 107: 33

"A fountain of gardens, a well of living waters, and streams from Lebanon."

- The Song of Solomon 4: 15

"For I will pour water upon him that is thirsty, and floods upon the dry ground: I will pour my spirit upon thy seed, and my blessing upon thine offspring."

- Isaiah 44: 3

"And they shall spring up *as* among the grass, as willows by the water courses."

- Isaiah 44: 4

"Let us draw near with a true heart in full assurance of faith, having our hearts sprinkled from an evil conscience, and our bodies washed with pure water."

- Hebrews 10: 22

Chapter 100

The Unjust Stewards

"BLESSINGS *are* upon the head of the just: but violence covereth the mouth of the wicked."

- Proverbs 10: 6

"For God shall bring every work into judgment, with every secret thing, whether *it be* good, or whether *it be* evil."

- Ecclesiastes 12: 14

"For of this sort are they which creep into houses, and lead captive silly women laden with sins, led away with divers lusts."

- 2 Timothy 3: 6

"Ever learning, and never able to come to the knowledge of the truth."

- 2 Timothy 3: 7

"But they shall proceed no further: for their folly shall be manifest unto all *men*, as theirs also was."

- 2 Timothy 3: 9

"He that is unjust, let him be unjust still: and he which is filthy, let him be filthy still: and he that is righteous, let him be righteous still: and he that is holy, let him be holy still."

- Revelation 22: 11

CHAPTER 101

THE TEMPLE

"CONCERNING this house which thou art in building, if thou wilt walk in my statutes, and execute my judgments, and keep all my commandments to walk in them; then will I perform my word with thee, which I spake unto David thy father."

- 1 Kings 6: 12

"And I will dwell among the children of Israel, and will not forsake my people Israel."

- 1 Kings 6: 13

"So Solomon built the house, and finished it."

- 1 Kings 6: 14

"And a man shall be as an hiding place from the wind, and a covert from the tempest; as rivers of water in a dry place, as the shadow of a great rock in a weary land."

- Isaiah 32: 2

"According to the grace of God which is given unto me, as a wise masterbuilder, I have laid the foundation, and another buildeth thereon. But let every man take heed how he buildeth thereupon."

- 1 Corinthians 3: 10

"For other foundation can no man lay than that is laid, which is Jesus Christ."

- 1 Corinthians 3: 11

"Every man's work shall be made manifest: for the day shall declare it, because it shall be revealed by fire; and the fire shall try every man's work of what sort it is."

- 1 Corinthians 3: 13

"If any man's work abide which he hath built thereupon, he shall receive a reward."

- 1 Corinthians 3: 14

"If any man's work shall be burned, he shall suffer loss: but he himself shall be saved; yet so as by fire."

- 1 Corinthians 3: 15

"In whom all the building fitly framed together groweth unto an holy temple in the Lord."

- Ephesians 2: 21

"Ye also, as lively stones, are built up a spiritual house, an holy priesthood, to offer up spiritual sacrifices, acceptable to God by Jesus Christ."

- 1 Peter 2: 5

Chapter 102

"HE restoreth my soul: he leadeth in the paths of righteousness for his name's sake."

- Psalms 23: 3

"The Lord redeemeth the soul of his servants: and none of them that trust in him shall be desolate."

- Psalms 34: 22

"O that my ways were directed to keep thy statutes!"

- Psalms 119: 5

"Are not five sparrows sold for two farthings, and not one of them is forgotten before God."

- Luke 12: 6

"But even the very hairs of your head are all numbered. Fear not therefore: ye are of more value than many sparrows."

- Luke 12: 7

Chapter 103

The Dyad

"SO God created man in his *own* image, in the image of God created he him; male and female created he them."

- Genesis 1: 27

"The voice of my beloved! behold, he cometh leaping upon the mountains, skipping upon the hills."

- The Song of Solomon 2: 8

"Thy two breasts *are* like two young roes that are twins, which feed among the lilies."

- The Song of Solomon 4: 5

"How fair and how pleasant art thou, O love, for delights. Come, my beloved, let us go forth into the field; let us lodge in the villages."

- The Song of Solomon 7: 6, 11

"That every one of you should know how to possess his vessel in sanctification and honour."

- 1 Thessalonians 4: 4

"Whereby are given unto us exceeding great and precious promises: that by these ye might be partakers of the divine nature, having escaped the corruption that is in the world through lust."

- 2 Peter 1: 4

Chapter 104

The Shepherd

"THE Lord *is* my shepherd; I shall not want."

- Psalms 23: 1

"He maketh me to lie down in green pastures: he leadeth me beside the still waters."

- Psalms 23: 2

"For the Son of Man is come to save that which was lost."

- Matthew 18: 11

"But he that entereth in by the door is the shepherd of the sheep."

- John 10: 2

"For ye were as sheep going astray; but are now returned unto the Shepherd and Bishop of your souls."

- 1 Peter 2: 25

"Behold, I stand at the door, and knock: if any man hear my voice, and open the door, I will come in to him, and will sup with him, and he with me."

- Revelation 3: 20

Chapter 105

The Herd

"THEY have mouths, but they speak not; eyes have they, but they see not."

- Psalms 135: 16

"He that turneth away his ear from hearing the law, even his prayer *shall be* abomination."

- Proverbs 28: 9

"And the Lord took me as I followed the flock, and the Lord said unto me, Go, prophesy unto my people Israel."

- Amos 7: 15

"Destruction and misery *are* in their ways."

- Romans 3: 16

"Denying ungodliness and worldly lusts, we should live soberly, righteously, and godly, in this present world."

- Titus 2: 12

"Beloved, follow not that which is evil, but that which is good. He that doeth good is of God: but he that doeth evil hath not seen God."

- 3 John 1: 11

"How long oh Lord, holy and true, dost thou not judge and avenge our blood on them that dwell on the earth?"

- Revelation 6: 10

Chapter 106

"A FOOL'S mouth *is* his destruction, and his lips *are* the snare of his soul."

- Proverbs 18: 7

"But when they persecute you in this city, flee ye into another."

- Matthew 10: 23

"Their throat *is* an open sepulchre; with their tongues they have used deceit; the poison of asps *is* under their lips."

- Romans 3: 13

"Whose mouth *is* full of cursing and bitterness."

- Romans 3: 14

"Who being past feeling have given themselves over unto lasciviousness, to work all uncleanness with greediness."

- Ephesians 4: 19

"For that righteous man dwelling among them, in seeing and hearing, vexed *his* righteous soul from day to day with their unlawful deeds."

- 2 Peter 2: 8

Chapter 107

The Thread

"AND if one prevail against him, two shall withstand him; and a threefold cord is not quickly broken."

- Ecclesiastes 4: 12

"Or ever the silvercord be loosed, or the golden bowl be broken, or the pitcher be broken at the fountain, or the wheel broken at the cistern."

- Ecclesiastes 12: 6

"Then shall the dust return to the earth as it was: and the spirit shall return unto God who gave it."

- Ecclesiastes 12: 7

"For we wrestle not against flesh and blood, but against principalities, against powers, against the rulers of the darkness of this world, against spiritual wickedness in high *places*."

- Ephesians 6: 12

"They are of the world: therefore speak they of the world, and the world heareth them."

- 1 John 4: 5

Chapter 108

The Rod of Iron

"YEA, though I walk through the valley of the shadow of death, I will fear no evil: for thou *art* with me; thy rod and thy staff they comfort me."

- Psalms 23: 4

"And there shall come forth a rod out of the stem of Jesse, and a Branch shall grow out of his roots."

- Isaiah 11: 1

"But with righteousness shall he judge the poor, and reprove with equity for the meek of the earth: and he shall smite the earth with the rod of his mouth, and with the breath of his lips shall he slay the wicked."

- Isaiah 11: 4

"Those things speak, and exhort, and rebuke with all authority. Let no man despise thee."

- Titus 2: 15

"Thou hast put all things in subjection under his feet. For in that he put all in subjection under him, he left nothing *that is* not put under him. But now we see not yet all things put under him."

- Hebrews 2: 8

"And he shall rule them with a rod of iron; as the vessels of a potter shall they be broken to shivers…"

- Revelation 2: 27

Chapter 109

The Wellspring

"AND David longed, and said, Oh that one would give me drink of the water of the well of Bethlehem, which *is* by the gate!"

- 2 Samuel 23: 15

"Understanding *is* a wellspring of life unto him that hath it: but the instruction of fools *is* folly."

- Proverbs 16: 22

"The words of a man's mouth *are as* deep waters, *and* the wellspring of wisdom *as* a flowing brook."

- Proverbs 18: 4

"Therefore with joy shall ye draw water out of the wells of salvation."

- Isaiah 12: 3

"Bless them which persecute you: bless, and curse not."

- Romans 12: 14

"Put them in mind to be subject to principalities and powers, to obey magistrates, to be ready to every good work."

- Titus 3: 1

Chapter 110

The Morning Star

"THERE shall come a Star out of Jacob, and a Scepter shall rise out of Israel, and shall smite the corners of Moab, and destroy all the children of Sheth."

- Numbers 24: 17

"And Nathan said to David, Thou *art* the man..."

- 2 Samuel 12: 7

"As the whirlwind passeth, so *is* the wicked no *more*: but the righteous *is* an everlasting foundation."

- Proverbs 10: 25

"For, lo, he that formeth the mountains, and created the wind, and declareth unto man what *is* his thought, that maketh the morning darkness, and treadeth upon the high places of the earth, The Lord, The God of hosts, *is* his name."

- Amos 4: 13

"For *it is* evident that our Lord sprang out of Juda: of which tribe Moses spake nothing concerning priesthood."

- Hebrews 7: 14

"I Jesus have sent mine angel to testify unto you these things in the churches, I am the root and the offspring of David, *and* the bright and morning star."

- Revelation 22: 16

CHAPTER 111

The King of Kings

"BUT whosoever shall deny me before men, him will I also deny before my Father which is in heaven."

- Matthew 10: 33

"All things are delivered unto me of my Father: and no man knoweth the Son, but the Father; neither knoweth any man the Father, save the Son, and *he* to whomsoever the Son will reveal *him*."

- Matthew 11: 27

"Who being the brightness of *his* glory, and the express image of his person, and upholding all things by the word of his power, when he had by himself purged our sins, sat down on the right hand of the Majesty on high."

- Hebrews 1: 3

"For this purpose the Son of God was manifested, that he might destroy the works of the devil."

- 1 John 3: 8

"Him that overcometh will I make a pillar in the temple of my God, and he shall go no more out: and I will write upon him the name of my God, and the name of the city of my God, *which is* new Jerusalem..."

- Revelation 3: 12

"And he hath on *his* vesture and on his thigh a name written, KING OF KINGS, AND LORD OF LORDS."

- Revelation 19: 16

Chapter 112

🌾 The Twelve Tribes of Israel 🌾

"SEEING that Abraham shall surely become a great and mighty nation, and all the nations of the earth shall be blessed in him."

- Genesis 18: 18

"And it came to pass after the death of Abraham, that God blessed his son Isaac..."

- Genesis 25: 11

"And Isaac called Jacob, and blessed him..."

- Genesis 28: 1

"And Jacob was left alone; and there wrestled a man with him until the breaking of the day."

- Genesis 32: 24

"And he said, Thy name shall be called no more Jacob, but Israel: for as a prince hast thou power with God and with men, and hast prevailed."

- Genesis 32: 28

"And Jacob called unto his sons, and said, Gather yourselves together, that I may tell you *that* which shall befall you in the last days."

- Genesis 49: 1

Chapter 113

The Israelites and the Philistines

"BEHOLD, it is come, and it is done, saith the Lord God; this *is* the day whereof I have spoken."

- Ezekiel 39: 8

"Woe unto you, scribes and Pharisees, hypocrites! because ye build the tombs of the prophets, and garnish the sepulchres of the righteous."

- Matthew 23: 29

"Wherefore ye be witnesses unto yourselves, that ye are the children of them which killed the prophets."

- Matthew 23: 31

"Who changed the truth of God into a lie, and worshipped and served the creature more than the Creator..."

- Romans 1: 25

"Neither murmur ye, as some of them also murmured, and were destroyed of the destroyer."

- 1 Corinthians 10: 10

"Ye have condemned *and* killed the just; *and* he doth not resist you."

- James 5: 6

Chapter 114

The Burning Cell

"IF one man sin against another, the judge shall judge him: but if a man sin against the Lord, who shall intreat for him?"

- 1 Samuel 2: 25

"Behold my servant, whom I have chosen; my beloved, in whom my soul is well pleased: I will put my spirit upon him, and he shall shew judgment to the gentiles."

- Matthew 12: 18

"For what is a man profited, if he shall gain the whole world, and lose his own soul? or what shall a man give in exchange for his soul?"

- Matthew 16: 26

"For men shall be lovers of their own selves, covetous, boasters, proud, blasphemers, disobedient to parents, unthankful, unholy. Without natural affection, trucebreakers, false accusers, incontinent, fierce, despisers of those that are good. Traitors, heady, highminded, lovers of pleasures more than lovers of God."

- 2 Timothy 3: 2, 3, 4

"And whosoever was not found written in the book of life was cast into the lake of fire."

- Revelation 20: 15

Chapter 115

The Persecution

"BLESSED *are* they which are persecuted for righteousness' sake: for theirs is the kingdom of heaven."

- Matthew 5: 10

"He must increase, but I must decrease."

- John 3: 30

"Yea, and all that will live godly in Christ Jesus shall suffer persecution."

- 2 Timothy 3: 12

"For consider him that endured such contradiction of sinners against himself, lest ye be wearied and faint in your minds."

- Hebrews 12: 3

"Marvel not, my brethren, if the world hate you."

- 1 John 3: 13

"And the dragon was wroth with the woman, and went to make war with the remnant of her seed, which keep the commandments of God, and have the testimony of Jesus Christ."

- Revelation 12: 17

Chapter 116

The Crucifixion

"BUT he *was* wounded for our transgressions, *he was* bruised for our iniquities: the chastisement of our peace *was* upon him; and with his stripes we are healed."

- Isaiah 53: 5

"Take my yoke upon you, and learn of me."

- Matthew 11: 29

"I am crucified with Christ: nevertheless I live; yet not I, but Christ liveth in me: and the life which I now live in the flesh I live by the faith of the Son of God, who loved me, and gave himself for me."

- Galatians 2: 20

"Who needeth not daily, as those high priests, to offer up sacrifices, first for his own sins; and then for the people's: for this he did once, when he offered up himself."

- Hebrews 7: 27

"Choosing rather to suffer affliction with the people of God, than to enjoy the pleasures of sin for a season."

- Hebrews 11: 25

"Whosoever believeth that Jesus is the Christ is born of God..."

- 1 John 5: 1

Chapter 117

THE FLAME

"AND the angel of the Lord appeared unto him in a flame of fire out of the midst of a bush: and he looked, and, behold, the bush burned with fire, and the bush *was* not consumed."

- Exodus 3: 2

"*I* AM the rose of Sharon, *and* the lily of the valleys."

- The Song of Solomon 2: 1

"But now once in the end of the world hath he appeared to put away sin by the sacrifice of himself."

- Hebrews 9: 26

"For all flesh *is* as grass, and all the glory of man as the flower of grass. The grass withereth, and the flower thereof falleth away."

- 1 Peter 1: 24

"But the word of the Lord endureth for ever. And this is the word which by the gospel is preached unto you."

- 1 Peter 1: 25

Chapter 118

The Death

"FOR since by man *came* death, by man *came* also the resurrection of the dead."

- 1 Corinthians 15: 21

"For as in Adam all die, even so in Christ shall all be made alive."

- 1 Corinthians 15: 22

"The last enemy *that* shall be destroyed *is* death."

- 1 Corinthians 15: 26

"But we see Jesus, who was made a little lower than the angels for the suffering of death, crowned with glory and honour; that he by the grace of God should taste death for every man."

- Hebrews 2: 9

"Forasmuch then as the children are partakers of flesh and blood, he also himself likewise took part of the same; that through death he might destroy him that had the power of death, that is, the devil."

- Hebrews 2: 14

"Knowing that shortly I must put off *this* my tabernacle, even as our Lord Jesus Christ hath shewed me."

- 2 Peter 1: 14

Chapter 119

The Sorrow

"YOUR iniquities have turned away these *things*, and your sins have withholden good *things* from you."

- Jeremiah 5: 25

"Then saith he unto them, My soul is exceeding sorrowful, even unto death: tarry ye here, and watch with me."

- Matthew 26: 38

"And he went a little further, and fell on his face, and prayed, saying, O my Father, if it be possible, let this cup pass from me: nevertheless not as I will, but as thou *wilt*."

- Matthew 26: 39

"But covet earnestly the best gifts: and yet shew I unto you a more excellent way."

- 1 Corinthians 12: 31

"Whose voice then shook the earth: but now he hath promised, saying, Yet once more I shake not the earth only, but also heaven."

- Hebrews 12: 26

CHAPTER 120

THE BREATH OF LIFE

"AND the Lord God formed man *of* the dust of the ground, and breathed into his nostrils the breath of life; and man became a living soul."

- Genesis 2: 7

"Thou hidest thy face, they are troubled: thou takest away their breath, they die, and return to their dust."

- Psalms 104: 29

"Let every thing that hath breath praise the Lord. Praise ye the Lord."

- Psalms 150: 6

"Thus saith the Lord God unto these bones; Behold, I will cause breath to enter into you, and ye shall live."

- Ezekiel 37: 5

"Then said he unto me, Prophesy unto the wind, prophesy, son of man, and say to the wind, Thus saith the Lord God; Come from the four winds, O breath, and breathe upon these slain, that they may live."

- Ezekiel 37: 9

Chapter 121

# The Resurrection

"AND have hope toward God, which they themselves also allow, that there shall be a resurrection of the dead, both of the just and unjust."

- Acts 24: 15

"Remember that Jesus Christ of the seed of David was raised from the dead according to my gospel."

- 2 Timothy 2: 8

"Therefore I endure all things for the elect's sakes, that they may also obtain the salvation which is in Christ Jesus with eternal glory."

- 2 Timothy 2: 10

"For by one offering he hath perfected for ever them that are sanctified."

- Hebrews 10: 14

"*I am* he that liveth, and was dead; and, behold, I am alive for evermore, Amen; and have the keys of hell and of death."

- Revelation 1: 18

"But the rest of the dead lived not again until the thousand years were finished. This *is* the first resurrection."

- Revelation 20: 5

Chapter 122

The Fallen Angels

"SUCH as sit in darkness and in the shadow of death, *being* bound in affliction and iron."

- Psalms 107: 10

"Because they rebelled against the words of God, and contemned the counsel of the most High."

- Psalms 107: 11

"How art thou fallen from heaven, O Lucifer, son of the morning! how art thou cut down to the ground, which didst weaken the nations!"

- Isaiah 14: 12

"And there was war in heaven: Michael and his angels fought against the dragon; and the dragon fought and his angels."

- Revelation 12: 7

"And prevailed not; neither was there place found any more in heaven."

- Revelation 12: 8

Chapter 123

The Last Antichrists

"AND every spirit that confesseth not that Jesus Christ is come in the flesh is not of God: and this is that *spirit* of antichrist, whereof ye have heard that it should come; and even now already is it in the world."

- 1 John 4: 3

"Raging waves of the sea, foaming out their own shame; wandering stars, to whom is reserved the blackness of darkness for ever."

- Jude 1: 13

"And the great dragon was cast out, that old serpent, called the Devil, and Satan, which deceiveth the whole world: he was cast out into the earth, and his angels were cast out with him."

- Revelation 12: 9

"And when the dragon saw that he was cast unto the earth, he persecuted the woman which brought forth the man *child*."

- Revelation 12: 13

Chapter 124

The End of Days

"AND the name of the star is called Wormwood: and the third part of the waters became wormwood; and many men died of the waters, because they were made bitter."

- Revelation 8: 11

"And they worshipped the dragon which gave power unto the beast: and they worshipped the beast, saying, Who *is* like unto the beast? Who is able to make war with him?"

- Revelation 13: 4

"And I beheld another beast coming up out of the earth; and he had two horns like a lamb, and he spake as a dragon."

- Revelation 13: 11

"And he exerciseth all the power of the first beast before him, and causeth the earth and them which dwell therein to worship the first beast, whose deadly wound was healed."

- Revelation 13: 12

"And he doeth great wonders, so that he maketh fire come down from heaven on the earth in the sight of men."

- Revelation 13: 13

Chapter 125

The False Prophet

"HIS confidence shall be rooted out of his tabernacle, and it shall bring him to the king of terrors."

- Job 18: 14

"Beware of false prophets, which come to you in sheep's clothing, but inwardly they are ravening wolves."

- Matthew 7: 15

"For there shall arise false Christs, and false prophets, and shall shew great signs and wonders; insomuch that, if it were possible, they shall deceive the very elect."

- Matthew 24: 24

"Beloved, believe not every spirit, but try the spirits whether they are of God: because many false prophets are gone out into the world."

- 1 John 4: 1

Chapter 126

The Battle of Armageddon

"AND this whole land shall be a desolation, *and* an astonishment..."

- Jeremiah 25: 11

"And the word of the Lord came unto me, saying, Son of man, set thy face against Gog, the land of Magog, the chief prince of Meshech and Tubal, and prophesy against Him."

- Ezekiel 38: 1, 2

"And say, Thus saith the Lord GOD; Behold, I *am* against thee, O Gog, the chief of Meshech and Tubal."

- Ezekiel 38: 3

"For the great day of his wrath is come; and who shall be able to stand?"

- Revelation 6: 17

"And the sixth angel sounded, and I heard a voice from the four horns of the golden alter which is before God."

- Revelation 9: 13

"Saying to the sixth angel which had the trumpet, Loose the four angels which are bound in the great river Euphrates."

- Revelation 9: 14

"And the four angels were loosed, which were prepared for an hour, and a day, and a month, and a year, for to slay the third part of men."

- Revelation 9: 15

"And the number of the army of the horsemen *were* two hundred thousand thousand: and I heard the number of them."

- Revelation 9: 16

"Here is wisdom. Let him that hath understanding count the number of the beast: for it is the number of a man; and his number *is* Six hundred threescore *and* six."

- Revelation 13: 18

"And I saw three unclean spirits like frogs *come* out of the mouth of the dragon, and out of the mouth of the beast, and out of the mouth of the false prophet."

- Revelation 16: 13

"For they are the spirits of devils, working miracles, *which* go forth unto the kings of the earth and of the whole world, to gather them to the battle of that great day of God Almighty."

- Revelation 16: 14

"And he gathered them together into a place called in the Hebrew tongue Armageddon."

- Revelation 16: 16

"And when the thousand years are expired, Satan shall be loosed out of his prison, And shall go out to deceive the nations which are in the four quarters of the earth, Gog and Magog, to gather them together to battle: the number of whom is as the sand of the sea."

- Revelation 20: 7, 8

Chapter 127

The Seven Headed Beast

"AND I stood upon the sand of the sea, and saw a beast rise up out of the sea, having seven heads and ten horns, and upon his horns ten crowns, and upon his heads the name of blasphemy."

- Revelation 13: 1

"And I saw one of his heads as it were wounded to death; and his deadly wound was healed: and all the world wondered after the beast."

- Revelation 13: 3

"And there was given unto him a mouth speaking great things and blasphemies; and power was given unto him to continue forty *and* two months."

- Revelation 13: 5

"And he causeth all, both small and great, rich and poor, free and bond, to receive a mark in their right hand, or in their foreheads."

- Revelation 13: 16

"And that no man might buy or sell, save he that had the mark, or the name of the beast, or the number of his name."

- Revelation 13: 17

Chapter 128

The Man and the Machine

"AND the man of thine, *whom* I shall not cut off from mine altar, *shall be* to consume thine eyes, and to grieve thine heart: and all the increase of thine house shall die in the flower of their age."

- 1 Samuel 2: 33

"Thou therefore endure hardness, as a good soldier of Jesus Christ."

- 2 Timothy 2: 3

"It is the last time: and as ye heard that antichrist shall come, even now there are many antichrists; whereby we know that it is the last time."

- 1 John 2: 18

"And they overcame him by the blood of the Lamb, and by the word of their testimony; and they loved not their lives unto the death."

- Revelation 12: 11

"And it was given unto him to make war with the saints, and to overcome them: and power was given him over all kindreds, and tongues, and nations."

- Revelation 13: 7

"And all that dwell upon the earth shall worship him, whose names are not written in the book of life of the Lamb slain from the foundation of the world."

- Revelation 13: 8

Chapter 129

The Flesh and Blood Hero

"FOR I know *that* my redeemer liveth, and *that* he shall stand at the latter *day* upon the earth."

- Job 19: 25

"For I have heard the slander of many: fear *was* on every side: while they took counsel together against me, they devised to take away my life."

- Psalms 31: 13

"If it be *so*, our God whom we serve is able to deliver us from the burning fiery furnace, and he will deliver *us* out of thine hand, O king."

- Daniel 3: 17

"But if not, be it known unto thee, O king, that we will not serve thy gods, nor worship the golden image which thou hast set up."

- Daniel 3: 18

"These are they which came out of the great tribulation, and have washed their robes, and made them white in the blood of the Lamb."

- Revelation 7: 14

Chapter 130

The Red Dragons of Death

"PULL me out of the net that they have laid privily for me: for thou *art* my strength."

- Psalms 31: 4

"For they bind heavy burdens and grievous to be borne, and lay *them* on men's shoulders; but they *themselves* will not move them with one of their fingers."

- Matthew 23: 4

"Ye serpents, *ye* generation of vipers, how can ye escape the damnation of hell?"

- Matthew 23: 33

"Behold, your house is left unto you desolate."

- Matthew 23: 38

"Likewise also these filthy dreamers, defile the flesh, despise dominion, and speak evil of dignities."

- Jude 1: 8

"And the dragon stood before the woman which was ready to be delivered, for to devour her child as soon as it was born."

- Revelation 12: 4

Chapter 131

The Four Horsemen of the Apocalypse

"BUT I will have mercy upon the house of Judah, and will save them by the Lord their God, and will not save them by bow, nor by sword, nor by battle, by horses, nor by horsemen."

- Hosea 2: 7

"For a nation is come up upon my land, strong, and without number, whose teeth *are* the teeth of a lion, and he hath the cheek teeth of a great lion."

- Joel 1: 6

"The vine is dried up, and the fig tree languisheth; the pomegranate tree, the palm tree also, and the apple tree, *even* all the trees of the field, are withered: because joy is withered away from the sons of men."

- Joel 1: 12

"Alas for the day! for the day of the Lord *is* at hand, and as a destruction from the Almighty shall it come."

- Joel 1: 15

"Is not the meat cut off before our eyes, *yea*, joy and gladness from the house of our God?"

- Joel 1: 16

"A day of darkness and of gloominess, a day of clouds and of thick darkness, as the morning spread upon the mountains: a great people and a strong; there hath not been ever the like, neither shall be any more after it, *even* to the years of many generations."

- Joel 2: 2

"A fire devoureth before them; and behind them a flame burneth: the land *is* as the garden of Eden before them, and behind them a desolate wilderness; yea, and nothing shall escape them."

- Joel 2: 3

"The appearance of them *is* as the appearance of horses; and as horsemen, so shall they run."

- Joel 2: 4

"Like the noise of chariots on the tops of mountains shall they leap, like the noise of a flame of fire that devoureth the stubble, as a strong people set in battle array."

- Joel 2: 5

"Before their face the people shall be much pained: all faces shall gather blackness."

- Joel 2: 6

Chapter 132

 The Tremors of Tribulation

"AND ye have this day rejected your God, who himself saved you out of all your adversities and your tribulations; and ye have said unto him, *Nay*, but set a king over us."

- 1 Samuel 10: 19

"He shall be driven from light into darkness, and chased out of the world."

- Job 18: 18

"Put them in fear, O Lord: *that* the nations may know themselves *to be but* men. Selah."

- Psalms 9: 20

"Your country *is* desolate, your cities *are* burned with fire: your land, strangers devour it in your presence, and *it is* desolate, as overthrown by strangers."

- Isaiah 1: 7

"How great *are* his signs! and how mighty *are* his wonders! his kingdom *is* an everlasting kingdom, and his dominion *is* from generation to generation."

- Daniel 4: 3

"He that is not with me is against me."

- Matthew 12: 30

"Oh ye hypocrites, ye can discern the face of the sky; but can ye not discern the signs of the times?"

- Matthew 16: 3

"Woe unto the world because of offences! For it must needs be that offences come; but woe to that man by whom offences cometh!"

- Matthew 18: 7

"Immediately after the tribulation of those days shall the sun be darkened, and the moon shall not give her light, and the stars shall fall from heaven, and the powers of the heavens shall be shaken."

- Matthew 24: 29

"For when they shall say, Peace and safety; then sudden destruction cometh upon them, as travail upon a woman with child; and they shall not escape."

- 1 Thessalonians 5: 3

"He that overcometh shall not be hurt of the second death."

- Revelation 2: 11

"And in those days shall men seek death, and shall not find it; and shall desire to die, and death shall flee from them."

- Revelation 9: 6

"Saying to them that dwell on the earth, that they should make an image to the beast, which had the wound by a sword, and did live."

- Revelation 13: 14

"And he had power to give life unto the image of the beast, that the image of the beast should both speak, and cause that as many as would not worship the image of the beast should be killed."

- Revelation 13: 15

Chapter 133

The Ascent to the Summit

"AND the Lord said, Behold, *there is* a place by me, and thou shalt stand upon a rock."

- Exodus 33: 21

"And it came to pass, as they still went on, and talked, that, behold, *there appeared* a chariot of fire, and horses of fire, and parted them both asunder; and Elijah went up by a whirlwind into heaven."

- 2 Kings 2: 11

"Who shall ascend into the hill of the Lord? Or who shall stand in his holy place?"

- Psalms 24: 3

"He that hath clean hands, and a pure heart; who hath not lifted up his soul unto vanity, nor sworn deceitfully."

- Psalms 24: 4

"Verily, verily, I say unto you, he that entereth not by the door into the sheepfold, but climbeth up some other way, the same is a thief and a robber."

- John 10: 1

Chapter 134

The Rescue of the Remnant

"IN a moment, in the twinkling of an eye, at the last trump: for the trumpet shall sound, and the dead shall be raised incorruptible, and we shall be changed."

- 1 Corinthians 15: 52

"Behold, he cometh with clouds; and every eye shall see him, and they *also* which pierced him: and all kindreds of the earth shall wail because of him. Even so, Amen."

- Revelation 1: 7

"And I looked, and behold a white cloud, and upon the cloud *one* sat like unto the Son of man, having on his head a golden crown, and in his hand a sharp sickle."

- Revelation 14: 14

"And another angel came out of the temple, crying with a loud voice to him that sat on the cloud, Thrust in thy sickle, and reap: for the time is come for thee to reap; for the harvest of the earth is *ripe*."

- Revelation 14: 15

"And he that sat on the cloud thrust in his sickle on the earth; and the earth was reaped."

- Revelation 14: 16

Chapter 135

The Wake of Destruction

"OR hath God assayed to go *and* take him a nation from the midst of *another* nation, by temptations, by signs, and by wonders, and by war, and by a mighty hand, and by a stretched out arm, and by great terrors, according to all that the Lord your God did for you in Egypt before your eyes?"

- Deuteronomy 4: 34

"How are the mighty fallen, and the weapons of war perished!"

- 2 Samuel 1: 27

"Thou turnest man to destruction..."

- Psalms 90: 3

"And when ye shall see Jerusalem compassed with armies, then know that the desolation thereof is nigh."

- Luke 21: 20

"But and if ye suffer for righteousness' sake, happy *are ye*: and be not afraid of their terror, neither be troubled."

- 1 Peter 3: 14

"Looking for and hasting unto the coming of the day of God, wherein the heavens being on fire shall be dissolved, and the elements shall melt with fervent heat."

- 2 Peter 3: 12

Chapter 136

The Mountain of God

"THE fear of the Lord *is* clean, enduring for ever: the judgments of the Lord *are* true *and* righteous altogether."

- Psalms 19: 9

"And it shall come to pass in the last days, *that* the mountain of the Lord's house shall be established in the top of the mountains, and shall be exalted above the hills; and all nations shall flow unto it."

- Isaiah 2: 2

"Now of the things which we have spoken *this is* the sum: We have such an high priest, who is set on the right hand of the throne of the Majesty in the heavens."

- Hebrews 8: 1

"By faith Noah, being warned of God of things not seen as yet, moved with fear, prepared an ark to the saving of his house; by the which he condemned the world, and became heir of the righteousness which is by faith."

- Hebrews 11: 7

"Who verily was foreordained before the foundation of the world, but was manifest in these last times for you."

- 1 Peter 1: 20

Chapter 137

The Sealed Book

"ALL scripture *is* given by inspiration of God, and *is* profitable for doctrine, for reproof, for correction, for instruction in righteousness."

- 2 Timothy 3: 16

"For the prophecy came not in old time by the will of man: but holy men of God spake *as they were* moved by the Holy Ghost."

- 2 Peter 1: 21

"And I saw another mighty angel come down from heaven, clothed with a cloud: and a rainbow *was* upon his head, and his face *was* as it were the sun, and his feet as pillars of fire."

- Revelation 10: 1

"And he had in his hand a little book open: and he set his right foot upon the sea, and *his* left *foot* on the earth."

- Revelation 10: 2

"And cried with a loud voice, as *when* a lion roareth: and when he had cried, seven thunders uttered their voices."

- Revelation 10: 3

"And sware by him that liveth for ever and ever, who created heaven, and the things that therein are, and the earth, and the things that therein are, and the sea, and the things which are therein, that there should be time no longer."

- Revelation 10: 6

Chapter 138

The Unsealed Book

"FOR he taught them as *one* having authority, and not as the scribes."

- Matthew 7: 29

"And I saw a strong angel proclaiming with a loud voice, Who is worthy to open the book, and to loose the seals thereof?"

- Revelation 5: 2

"And no man in heaven, nor in earth, neither under the earth, was able to open the book, neither to look thereon."

- Revelation 5: 3

"And I wept much, because no man was found worthy to open and to read the book, neither to look thereon."

- Revelation 5: 4

"And one of the elders saith unto me, Weep not: behold, the Lion of the tribe of Juda, the Root of David, hath prevailed to open the book, and to loose the seven seals thereof."

- Revelation 5: 5

"And the fifth angel sounded, and I saw a star fall from heaven unto the earth: and to him was given the key of the bottomless pit."

- Revelation 9: 1

Chapter 139

The Inner Vision

"HAVE mercy upon me, O Lord, for I am in trouble: mine eye is consumed with grief, *yea*, my soul and my belly."

- Psalms 31: 9

"The burden of the valley of vision. What aileth thee now, that thou art wholly gone up to the housetops?"

- Isaiah 22: 1

"The light of the body is the eye: If therefore thine eye be single, thy whole body shall be full of light."

- Matthew 6: 22

"While we look not at the things which are seen, but at the things which are not seen: for the things which are seen *are* temporal; but the things which are not seen *are* eternal."

- 2 Corinthians 4: 18

"That he would grant you, according to the riches of his glory, to be strengthened with might by his spirit in the inner man."

- Ephesians 3: 16

"Follow peace with all *men*, and holiness, without which no man shall see the Lord."

- Hebrews 12: 14

Chapter 140

The Law Divine

"THE law of the Lord *is* perfect, converting the soul: the testimony of the Lord *is* sure, making wise the simple."

- Psalms 19: 7

"Gilead *is* mine, and Manasseh *is* mine; Ephraim also *is* the strength of mine head; Judah *is* my lawgiver."

- Psalms 60: 7

"O Lord, I know that the way of man *is* not in himself: *it is* not in man that walketh to direct his steps."

- Jeremiah 10: 23

"Wherefore then *serveth* the law? It was added because of transgressions, till the seed should come to whom the promise was made; *and it was* ordained by angels in the hand of the mediator."

- Galatians 3: 19

"For all the law is fulfilled in one word, *even* in this; Thou shalt love thy neighbor as thyself."

- Galatians 5: 14

"There is one lawgiver, who is able to save and to destroy: who art thou that judgest another."

- James 4: 12

Chapter 141

The Power Supreme

"THAT Christ may dwell in your hearts by faith; that ye, being rooted and grounded in love."

- Ephesians 3: 17

"May be able to comprehend with all saints what *is* the breadth, and length, and depth, and height."

- Ephesians 3: 18

"And to know the love of Christ, which passeth knowledge, that ye might be filled with all the fulness of God."

- Ephesians 3: 19

"For by him were all things created, that are in heaven, and that are in earth, visible and invisible, whether *they be* thrones, or dominions, or principalities, or powers: all things were created by him, and for him."

- Colossians 1: 16

"For this is the message that ye heard from the beginning, that we should love one another."

- 1 John 3: 11

"There is no fear in love; but perfect love casteth out fear: because fear hath torment. He that feareth is not made perfect in love."

- 1 John 4: 18

Chapter 142

The Blessing of Israel

"AND I will make them and the places round about my hill a blessing; and I will cause the shower to come down in his season; there shall be showers of blessing."

- Ezekiel 34: 26

"Ye which have followed me, in the regeneration when the Son of man shall sit in the throne of his glory, ye also shall sit upon twelve thrones, judging the twelve tribes of Israel."

- Matthew 19: 28

"And, behold, I send the promise of my Father upon you: but tarry ye in the city of Jerusalem, until ye be endued with power from on high."

- Luke 24: 49

"And he led them out as far as to Bethany, and he lifted up his hands, and blessed them."

- Luke 24: 50

"And it came to pass, while he blessed them, he was parted from them, and carried up into heaven."

- Luke 24: 51

"And they worshipped him, and returned to Jerusalem with great joy."

- Luke 24: 52

Chapter 143

The True Human

"THEN came Jesus forth, wearing the crown of thorns, and the purple robe. And *Pilate* saith unto them, Behold the man!"

- John 19: 5

"For what man knoweth the things of a man, save the spirit of man which is in him? even so the things of God knoweth no man, but the spirit of God."

- 1 Corinthians 2: 11

"But when that which is perfect is come, then that which is in part shall be done away."

- 1 Corinthians 13: 10

"And above all these things *put on* charity, which is the bond of perfectness."

- Colossians 3: 14

"That the man of God may be perfect, throughly furnished unto all good works."

- 2 Timothy 3: 17

"Wherefore in all things it behoved him to be made like unto *his* brethren, that he might be a merciful and faithful high priest in things *pertaining* to God, to make reconciliation for the sins of the people."

- Hebrews 2: 17

Chapter 144

The Crown of Life

"THESE things I have spoken unto you, that in me ye might have peace. In the world ye shall have tribulation: but be of good cheer; I have overcome the world."

- John 16: 33

"Therefore, my brethren dearly beloved and longed for, my joy and crown, so stand fast in the Lord, *my* dearly beloved."

- Philippians 4: 1

"I have fought a good fight, I have finished *my* course, I have kept the faith."

- 2 Timothy 4: 7

"For whatsoever is born of God overcometh the world: and this is the victory that overcometh the world, *even* our faith."

- 1 John 5: 4

"To him that overcometh will I give to eat of the tree of life, which is in the midst of the paradise of God."

- Revelation 2: 7

"Be thou faithful unto death, and I will give thee a crown of life."

- Revelation 2: 10

"And I will give him the morning star."

- Revelation 2: 28

"Did Anyone Hear?"

"Did Anyone Understand?"

"The Puzzle Persists!"

Permissions, Citations & Acknowledgments

GRATEFUL ACKNOWLEDGMENT and HEARTFELT THANKS are made to the following:

The Crown, the Syndics at Cambridge University Press and L. Nicol, Permissions Manager, for permission to use excerpts from the "Holy Bible."

"Extracts from the Authorized Version of the Bible (The King James Bible), the rights in which are vested in the Crown, are reproduced by permission of the Crown's Patentee, Cambridge University Press."

GRATEFUL ACKNOWLEDGMENT and RECOGNITION is made to the following:

To Penguin Group (USA) Inc., Michael Drosnin, Eliyahu Rips, and F. B. Eichin, Permissions Manager, for the authorization to reprint passages from Michael Drosnin's book, "Bible Code II, The Countdown," published by Penguin Books, 2003.

Passage taken from: Coda, Page 239, First Paragraph, as follows: "Sir Isaac Newton, was certain that not only the Bible, but the entire universe, was a "cryptogram set by the Almighty," a puzzle that God made, and that we were meant to solve." Reprinted in this volume in: Author's Note, Page vii, First Paragraph.

Passage taken from: Coda, Page 240, Last Paragraph, as follows: "In any event, it seems that the object we need, both to survive, and to gain the final insight, is the "code key" buried in Lisan." Reprinted in this volume in: Chapter 138, Page 189, Fifth Paragraph.

GRATEFUL ACKNOWLEDGMENT and TRIBUTE is made to the following:

To Taylor & Francis Books Ltd., Curzon Press Ltd., Christmas Humphreys, and H. Sanders, Permissions & Subsidiary Rights Administrator, for permission to reprint passages from Christmas Humphreys' book, "Karma and Rebirth," published by Curzon Press, 1983.

Passage taken from: Chapter One, Page 28, Last Paragraph, as follows: "Paracelsus wrote, "Philosophy is only the true perception and understanding of Cause and Effect." Reprinted in this volume in: Chapter 55, Page 75, First Paragraph.

Passage taken from: Chapter Two, Page 38, Last Paragraph, as follows: "Man is punished by his sins, not for them." Reprinted in this volume in: Chapter 34, Page 54, First Paragraph.

———⟫●⟪———

GRATEFUL ACKNOWLEDGMENT and MUCH APPRECIATION are made to the following:

"The Bible Code: Predicting Armageddon." Format: DVD-Video, Region 1. History Channel. DVD Release Date: September 7, 2003. Cited in this volume in: Chapter 138, Page 188, First Six Paragraphs & Chapter 138, Page 189, Third Paragraph.

"Bible Code II: Apocalypse and Beyond." Format: DVD-Video, Region 1. History Channel. DVD Release Date: April 11, 2004. Cited in this volume in: Chapter 138, Page 189, First & Second Paragraphs.

"Mayan Doomsday Prophecy." Format: DVD-Video, Region 1. History Channel. DVD Release Date: August 3, 2006. Cited in this volume in: Chapter 88, Page 121, First Paragraph.

"Doomsday 2012: The End of Days." Format: DVD-Video, Region 1. History Channel. DVD Release Date: March 1, 2007. Cited in this volume in: Chapter 88, Page 121, Third Paragraph.

"The Lost Book of Nostradamus." Format: DVD-Video, Region 1. History Channel. DVD Release Date: October 28, 2007. Cited in this volume in: Chapter 88, Page 121, Second & Sixth Paragraphs.

Wikipedia.org. "Last Prophet." 01 April 2009. Online Encyclopedia. Accessed on 01 June 2009. <http://en.wikipedia.org/wiki/Last_prophet/>. Cited in this volume in: Definitions and Terms, Page 202, Third & Fourth Terms.

———⟫●⟪———

GRATEFUL ACKNOWLEDGMENT with DEEP AFFECTION is made to the following:

Queensryche. "Promised Land." Prod. Queensryche and James Barton. Label: EMI America. Genre: Heavy Metal, Progressive Metal. Format: Studio Album, CD. Original Release Date: October 18, 1994. Cited in this volume in: Chapter 68, Page 95, Fifth Paragraph.

About the Author

DALE LAWSON, a messenger, a prophet, One Male, a mystery indeed, but surely he is the last of the metaphysicians of our age. He arrives and exhorts in the tradition of the Hebrew prophets of old and heralds the end of the "Word of God" for this era. Forsaking a conventional role in favor of following his own spiritual path, he has studied history, philosophy, psychology and religion. Standing apart, however from formal affiliation to any one sect, he is inclined toward a Zen approach to life, in principle and as a matter of practical living. He remains open to the truth wherever it may be found. He is an immovable witness in a Monotheistic God. From the One come many, and like the rivers return to the sea, the many return to the One! He lives in Southern California.

WRITE TO THE AUTHOR

BOTH the author and publisher appreciate hearing from you and learning of your experience with this book and how it has served you. All mail addressed to the author is forwarded but it should be understood that "The Last Prophet" will not generally reply to all the mail he receives. He reserves the right of reply but the sender must cover the expense in U.S. funds for a reply to be considered, the sender should also be a legitimate buyer of the book. However, your letter will be read by "The Last Prophet" and he can intercede on your behalf and he will record your name in his "Book of Saints!" Any reply is for personal enrichment, fulfillment and insight and are non-binding on the author or publisher in any way.

You can write to "The Last Prophet" and share your thoughts or concerns, share your hopes and dreams, submit a photo or a prayer request, send a letter of thanks, a recommendation of the book, a word of praise or a gift of support for this work and this message, and we will forward your request. You may write to:

DALE LAWSON
C/O LAST DAYS PRESS
P.O. BOX 83657
SAN DIEGO, CA 92138 U.S.A.

www.ingramcontent.com/pod-product-compliance
Lightning Source LLC
Chambersburg PA
CBHW022101150426
43195CB00008B/220